Developing Counselling, edited by Windy Dryden, is an innovative series of books which provides counsellors and counselling trainees with practical hints and guidelines on the problems they face in the counselling process. The books assume that readers have a working knowledge of the approach in question, and, in a clear and accessible fashion show how the counsellor can more effectively translate that knowledge into everyday practice.

Books in the series include:

Developing the Practice of Counselling
Windy Dryden and Colin Feltham

Developing Counsellor Supervision
Colin Feltham and Windy Dryden

Developing Counsellor Training
Windy Dryden and Colin Feltham

Developing Psychodynamic Counselling
Brendan McLoughlin

Developing Rational Emotive Behavioural Counselling
Windy Dryden and Joseph Yankura

Developing Cognitive-Behavioural Counselling
Michael J. Scott, Stephen G. Stradling and Windy Dryden

Developing Transactional Analysis Counselling
Ian Stewart

Developing Gestalt Counselling
Jennifer Mackewn

Developing
Person-Centred
Counselling

Second Edition

Dave Mearns

SAGE Publications
London • Thousand Oaks • New Delhi

First edition published 1994. Reprinted 1996 (twice), 1998, 2000, 2002
Second edition first published 2003

SAGE Publications Ltd
6 Bonhill Street
London EC2A 4PU

SAGE Publications Inc
2455 Teller Road
Thousand Oaks, California 91320

SAGE Publications India Pvt Ltd
32, M-Block Market
Greater Kailash – I
New Delhi 110 048

British Library Cataloguing in Publication Data

A catalogue record for this book is available
from the British Library

ISBN 0 7619 4968 2
ISBN 0 7619 4969 0 (pbk)

Library of Congress Control Number available

Typeset by M Rules
Printed and bound in Great Britain by TJ International Ltd, Padstow, Cornwall

Maria Villas Bowen

This book is dedicated to Maria Bowen. Maria was a Brazilian psychologist who became an integral member of the Center for Studies of the Person in La Jolla during Carl Rogers' years there. Indeed, Maria was one of Carl's most valued friends and colleagues – someone with whom he loved to engage in theoretical debate. Maria was also a therapist who had a considerable reputation – one of her clients said 'She had such a huge personality that there was room for everyone'.

I knew Maria from 1971 to 1994 when she died of AIDS. A year later her husband Jack Bowen, another of my friends, died similarly.

Dave Mearns
April 2002

Contents

IV The Therapeutic Process

V Person-Centred Psychopathology

Preface to the Second Edition

Historically, the first edition of *Developing Person-Centred Counselling* (1994) was positioned after *Person-Centred Counselling in Action* (1998 and 1999, co-authored with Brian Thorne) and just before *Person-Centred Counselling Training* (1997). The intention was to offer an extension to thinking about person-centred counselling beyond the introduction offered in *Person-Centred Counselling in Action*. Thereafter, *Person-Centred Counselling Training* deepened exposition on the development of the person-centred specialist. More recently *Person-Centred Therapy Today* (2000, with Brian Thorne) seeks to reflect its title and introduce the very edges of the approach including work on 'Configuration Theory' and the revision of Rogers' Self Theory. These four texts do not duplicate one another – each has a place sequentially in the development of the person-centred counsellor.

This second edition retains most of the sections from the original book, though all have been revised, some extensively, to reflect developments in the past eight years. Only two sections have been completely dropped. The section 'How to work with a couple?' has been superseded by two good books on person-centred couple and family therapy by Charles O'Leary (1999) and Ned Gaylin (2001). The section 'How much of your "self" can you use therapeutically with your client?' is dropped because similar material now appears in chapter 7 of *Person-Centred Therapy Today* (Mearns and Thorne, 2000). These sections have been replaced by 'Don't get "hooked on growth"' and 'Getting beyond "transference"'. The first has proved to be of great practical value to counsellors – it shows how easy it is to miss the parts of the client whose impetus appears to be oppositely directed to 'growth'. The 'transference' section gives a modern appraisal of 'transference process' and its place in person-centred counselling.

In total, 6000 words and 50 references have been added to the book in this second edition, but it is still written as a thoroughly practical text – one which offers 30 focused seminars to help the person-centred counsellor to develop her practice.

The first edition sold 15 000 copies, considerably more than were expected by the publisher. Part of this popularity is its positioning in the sequence of four, but a lot has to do with the style of writing which attempts to communicate complex ideas simply and also to retain in its writing that most important ingredient of person-centred counselling – its attention to the humanity of the endeavour.

Dave Mearns
April, 2002

Introduction

The person-centred counsellor must always remember that she is a guest within the client's world of experience. This first sentence encapsulates the 'essence' of person-centred counselling. Most other approaches to counselling and therapy are much more exciting for the counsellor and perhaps also for the client with the practitioner playing a dashing role exhibiting mastery of sophisticated skills of analysis, interpretation and near mystical insight into the client's condition and requirements for change. Compared to this exciting portrayal the person-centred counsellor presents a somewhat quieter image.

In many ways person-centred counselling does not fit so-called Western culture where the notion of being helped to heal oneself is attractive only in the margins of society and where expertness in the pursuit of authority over others is a goal at every level of societal functioning from commerce through academia to the criminal fraternity.

It is commonly supposed that the person-centred approach has no goals for the client beyond that which the client has for himself. This is of course nonsense. There is at least an implicit aim behind all person-centred working: that, under certain conditions, the 'client' will be helped to find and to exercise more of his own personal power with regard to understanding and evaluating his actions in the past and present and in making decisions for the future. Furthermore, it is expected that this gain will, in some degree, carry forward to be exercised by the client in his future life. This implicit aim of the person-centred approach renders it unsuitable and even dangerous in contexts where the authority is seeking to develop and maintain a 'social control' function over the client.

Perhaps the most central concept in the person-centred approach is *conditions of worth*. Throughout the socialisation of the child he is faced with the fact that his worth as defined by other people is dependent on whether he measures up to particular conditions. If these conditions for his worth are particularly oppressive, inconsistent or ambiguous the roots will be laid for difficulty in adulthood as he attempts valiantly but in vain to live up to the conditions. Sometimes the difficulty which the person experiences in adulthood is only indirectly related to the conditions of worth but more to do with the way the young person *adjusted* his or her living to exist within the constraints of the conditions. In other words, the very adjustments which the person made to survive difficult early circumstances might become the source of later problems as those adjustments fail to work effectively in adult life. In a sense, he is struggling to 'survive his survival'. These two factors: the conditions of worth and the ways in which the person has adjusted to the conditions of worth are the main ways in which 'maladjustment' is understood within the person-centred approach.

Another central concept which follows on from conditions of worth is *locus of evaluation*: the degree to which the person can be his own locus of evaluation or whether that locus of evaluation is externalised with the person unable to make judgements about himself but reliant on the judgements of others. The way a person-centred counsellor works will vary considerably according to the extent to which the client's locus of evaluation is *externalised* or *internalised* (see Sections 19 and 20). As mentioned earlier, an implicit aim of person-centred working is to help the client to internalise his locus of evaluation. Helping another person to internalise his locus of evaluation is not achieved by exercising power over him but by creating a relationship in which the client may take responsibility for himself. The singular genius of Carl Rogers, the founder of the approach, was in enunciating and evaluating the relationship conditions in which that client empowerment might be optimised. Rogers laid down six such *therapeutic conditions*. Currently the most accessible account of these conditions is presented in Kirschenbaum and Henderson (1989: 221).

> For constructive personality change to occur, it is necessary that these conditions exist and continue over a period of time:
>
> 1. Two persons are in psychological contact.
> 2. The first, whom we shall term the client, is in a state of incongruence, being vulnerable or anxious.
> 3. The second person, whom we shall term the therapist, is congruent or integrated in the relationship.
> 4. The therapist experiences unconditional positive regard for the client.
> 5. The therapist experiences an empathic understanding of the client's internal frame of reference and endeavours to communicate this experience to the client.
> 6. The communication to the client of the therapist's empathic understanding and unconditional positive regard is to a minimal degree achieved.

The strength of Rogers' theory was in this clear statement of the central hypotheses, and considerable research ensued to confirm the importance of the third, fourth and fifth conditions on the congruence, unconditional positive regard and empathy offered by the counsellor (Mearns, 1993a) as well as the relevance of the sixth condition on the communication of these to the client. It must be said that the first condition was largely taken for granted until the work of Garry Prouty and Dion Van Werde pointed out that psychological 'contact' could not be presumed with clients whose difficulties were more profound. This observation led to the more recent development of client-centred 'pre-therapy' for work with clients whose 'contact' with their affect and with other people is impaired (see Sections 29 and 30 of this book).

The strength of Rogers' theory in presenting clear hypotheses has, paradoxically, led to a difficulty of interpretation. Because empathy and unconditional positive regard could be clearly defined, the naive presumption has developed that a simple *portrayal* of these conditions is what is required of the person-centred counsellor. New students of person-centred counselling and those who are trained by non-specialists in the approach often labour under the misapprehension that all they need to do is to exhibit empathy and unconditional positive regard. The student in these circumstances is thrown into some degree of chaos by the simultaneous demand for congruence. The problem is that conditions such as empathy and unconditional positive regard cannot be 'portrayed' towards a client with any degree of effectiveness: clients are not so easily fooled by incongruent portrayal. The task then for the developing person-centred counsellor is quite momentous – she has to *become* the kind of counsellor who genuinely feels a deep *valuing* and *interest* towards her clients, no matter how varied the clients may be. This heralds the true challenge of person-centred training: the enormous personal development work which is necessary to win a sufficient degree of *self-acceptance* to allow the counsellor to feel consistently unthreatened, accepting and open to the experiencing of her clients.

This book does not go into detail on any of the above aspects of person-centred theory and practice but assumes that the reader will have familiarity with these basics. The reader is referred to the earlier Sage publication: *Person-Centred Counselling in Action*, second edition (Mearns and Thorne, 1999) for a thorough grounding in the approach. The present book has been compiled in such a way as to offer no duplication with that earlier text but to invite the reader to explore the middle reaches of the approach.

The first part of the book, 'Extending the Therapeutic Conditions', offers thoughts and practical examples of ways in which the experienced person-centred counsellor can function *fully* as a person in the thera-peutic endeavour. Much of this section presumes considerable personal and professional development on the part of the counsellor. Some aspects of that development are explored in the second part of the book, 'The Development of the Counsellor', including the crises which commonly hit person-centred counsellors during training like 'paralysis' and the need to feel 'clever'. Highly practical advice is also given on the handling of difficult personal material aroused during training. Part III, entitled 'The Therapeutic Alliance', includes fairly detailed exploration of the intricacies and depths of the therapeutic relationship, even the 'unspoken' tracts of that relationship. One of the chief areas of interest for the author is the exploration of 'The Therapeutic Process' within person-centred working. This forms Part IV of the book with a contribution by Brian Thorne on short-term person-centred counselling and other sections exploring the centrality of the 'power dynamic' and 'locus of evaluation' in person-centred work. Part IV also includes theoretical suggestions on the nature of self-concept change and how that may induce apparent 'stuckness' and regression in the therapeutic process. The fifth and final part of the book is perhaps the most important in offering areas for future development: 'Person-Centred Psychopathology' has been a very neglected dimension for person-centred work but this section offers considerable new thinking in four chapters by Elke Lambers, who was set the task of addressing traditional psychodiagnostic categories in terms of person-centred theory. The person-centred approach has long had an uneasy relationship with psychodiagnostic terms, which it rightly regards as unnecessary and even somewhat obtru-sive in relating to the individual client. However, it is important for the person-centred counsellor to be able to relate with these terms if she is to function within a clinical setting. The last two sections of the book are provided by Dion Van Werde on client-centred 'pre-therapy' developed initially by Garry Prouty as a way of working with clients who have severe problems in maintaining 'contact' with their own affect and with other people. Pre-therapy is one of the most important developments in the last twenty years of person-centred work, offering as it does a mean-ingful basis for working with largely neglected client groups. The other major development, the work of Margaret Warner on 'fragile' and 'disso-ciated' processes is not included in this text because it is well-described elsewhere (Warner, 2000; Warner, 2002b)

   This introduction needs to contain some paragraphs on *language*. Frequent mention during the book is given to 'the training period' without that term ever being defined. The author considers that the training period for a person-centred counsellor is somewhere between three and five years, regardless of the length of the actual training course, which tends to vary from one year full-time to three years part-time. Whether that basic training is completed within one year of completely intensive work or three years during which the work can be better integrated with practice, there should still follow some years during which the counsellor is in an embryonic phase as a person-centred practitioner.

This book tends to use the term 'person-centred counsellor' rather than the more common 'person-centred therapist'. The reason for this choice is simply one of maintaining consistency within the series. The training of the person-centred practitioner seeks to equip her to function at whatever depths are required by each new client. Whether that work should be called 'counselling', 'therapy' or 'psychotherapy' is largely irrelevant. While the term 'counsellor' is predominantly used in this text, Sections 29 and 30 respect the convention of the author's cultural context by using 'therapist'.

The same policy is adopted for the use of *pronouns* as that which has been well received in *Person-Centred Counselling in Action*, second edition (Mearns and Thorne, 1999): within the general text the counsellor is 'she' and the client is 'he'. Obvious exceptions to this exist in some of the reproduced case material, where to change the sex of the client or the counsellor might radically alter the material. Also, the female pronoun is used for the client in Section 26 on 'borderline personality disorder' simply because this experience is only rarely found in men.

This text does not seek to be *politically correct* in terms of the choice of material or the language which is currently prevalent in Britain. The reader should note that political correctness is very much tied to specific cultures, and language which would not be 'correct' in Britain might be the norm elsewhere. This particularly applies to some of the terms used in the pre-therapy sections (29 and 30). It was deemed to be disrespectful to change language which was perfectly appropriate in the culture from which it originated. This issue of political correctness was also considered in relation to the material presented in Section 20. Some consultations suggested that the client material described in this section should not be published lest it give the impression that accounts of the sexual abuse of infants and ritualised sexual abuse are over-emphasised. The author decided not to censor this material on those grounds but wishes to make it clear that he is of the opinion that these abuses are if anything under-estimated rather than over-estimated in modern society.

The book contains a considerable amount of client material. Extreme care has been taken to preserve both the confidentiality and the anonymity of the clients. Permission has been obtained to reproduce any parts which could have been identifiable by the client himself and changes have also been made to ensure that there are no features which might be identified by other persons. Furthermore, a strict policy has been observed of not using material from clients with whom work was current at the time of writing. Although clients are usually quite happy that such material be used, it can have unforeseen effects upon the therapeutic relationship.

With all these introductions and cautions expressed, let us embark upon a journey round thirty critical and at times controversial issues at the forefront of thinking in the practice of person-centred counselling – where better to begin than with the perhaps controversial suggestion that 'unconditional positive regard' has little to do with 'liking'!

Gordon, R
Collect By 22 Mar 2024
Romsey

Reserved item

Branch: Romsey
Date: 8/03/2024   **Time**:   11:21 AM
Name: Gordon, Rachel

Item: Developing person-centred counselling
C014990088

Expires: 22 Mar 2024

I

Extending the
Therapeutic Conditions

1 Don't confuse unconditional positive regard with 'liking'

The most frequent question posed by new students of person-centred counselling is '*How can I possibly like all my clients?*'

Typically, trainers field this question by pointing to how the training process helps to establish a more open, less self-protective disposition in the counsellor, who then has less need to respond judgementally to clients. As the expressions of the new trainees begin to glaze over with incomprehension the trainer may deepen her explanation by embarking on a description of the gradual development of self-acceptance which accompanies an effective training process and the impact which that change has on the counsellor's openness to accept others. By the time this lecture is finished the wilting trainee nods meekly, not in acknowledgement of understanding, but in submission to the punishment which has followed the asking of such a difficult question. After the session the trainee may be heard muttering to a fellow student, 'But I still don't understand how you can like all your clients!'

The reason for the difficulty behind this question is that the trainee and the trainer have been talking about different things. The trainee has been talking about *liking* and the trainer has been explaining the development of the attitude of *unconditional positive regard*. Unfortunately, these two concepts do not have much in common between them. Customarily the human being is highly selective in the people to whom he or she attributes liking. Usually this attribution is made on the basis of a perceived similarity in values or complementarity of needs. It is unlikely that more than a minority of the counsellor's clients will exhibit similar values and complementarity of needs may extend no further than the need to receive counselling and the need to offer it. Indeed, in those few instances where the counsellor experiences a strong similarity in values or complementarity of needs, she might rightly feel caution on the grounds that this is fertile ground for over-involvement with the client.

Unconditional positive regard is unrelated to any similarity of values or complementarity of needs with the client. Unconditional positive regard is about the counsellor *valuing* the client in his or her totality. The counsellor will not only value the parts of the client that are struggling to achieve a more satisfying and meaningful existence but also the many self-protective screens which the client has erected to distance himself from the feared threat posed by other people. Here lies the central therapeutic power of the dimension: its unconditionality contradicts the *conditions of worth* which have restricted the client's growth (Lietaer, 1984). This unconditionality is so rare in our cultures that clients as well as new trainees may have difficulty in trusting it, as shown by one client:

> For a long while I gave Catriona [his counsellor] the same hard time as I gave everyone else who threatened to get close to me. I eyed her with distrust, tried to convince myself that she was only 'acting' and challenged her at every opportunity. I guess I was testing out whether the interest she was showing in me was genuine or yet another clever manipulation. After a while I found that I was believing it and from then on I behaved more reasonably towards her, but that was pretty scary – for a long time I kept hold of an elastic attached to my nice, safe cynicism.

Unconditional positive regard is an extremely difficult attitude to develop. As has been detailed elsewhere (Mearns and Thorne, 1999; Mearns, 1997a), it involves the counsellor in considerable personal development work to attain a level of personal security and self-acceptance which reduces her need to protect self against others. Unless that extensive personal development work takes place any 'display' of unconditional positive regard on the part of the counsellor tends to be superficial and usually wilts under the challenge of well-developed client self-protective systems. Indeed, this superficial portrayal of unconditional positive regard is usually no better than 'liking' in that it is highly selective: the counsellor finds it possible to portray it towards certain clients who exhibit a similarity of values, but not to others who are different from her.

For the person-centred counsellor, unconditional positive regard is about *being* rather than *portraying*. The consistent valuing of clients stems from the fact that the counsellor has come to be less threatened by others and can prize rather than feel fearful about their differences.

As described in the earlier quote, for a time the client may be as suspicious of the counsellor's '*liking*' as the trainee who posed the original question. Clients also know that liking is usually related to similarities and complementarities. Hopefully, as the counselling progresses, they will experience the power of being valued for all that they are rather than simply being liked for some of what they are.

> **KEY POINT** 'Liking' is not at all the same as *unconditional positive regard*. The latter depends on the counsellor's achievement of self-acceptance and cannot simply be 'portrayed'.

2 Offering the client an engagement at 'relational depth'

Doing a counselling 'demo' in front of 30 course members and a video camera adds something of an 'edge' to the activity. The public arena was not particularly conducive to intimate relating but what I wanted to do was to offer the 'client', Terry, a quality of engagement that might allow him to meet me at 'relational depth'. It is this depth of relating that distinguishes the person-centred approach from others. It is qualitatively different from work that is focused upon 'transference', which occurs at a much more superficial level of relationship (Mearns, 2002a). If the client feels convinced of the counsellor's ability and willingness to meet him at relational depth he may experience the safety and companionship that allows him to enter his existential processes and share that world with the counsellor. Here he shares his very existence as he is experiencing it – the fundamental needs, fears, conflicts, the utter desolation and the life-giving hope. This is the territory which is life itself – which he would yearn to share as strongly as he would fear to share. In this territory he does not talk *about* his experiencing – he *is* his experiencing. He does not seek to protect his self from being seen either by the counsellor or by himself. In his existential process he cannot lie – lying belongs to a much more superficial level of relating. This is what makes person-centred counselling different – its extraordinary depth of human contact (Mearns, 1996; Mearns, 1997a: chapter 2; Mearns and Thorne, 2000: chapter 5; Mearns, 2002a; Mearns, 2002c).

The session lasted 40 minutes during which I had been able to relax sufficiently to be fully present with Terry in the sense that I was not self-consciously thinking about how to be with him or how to respond to him, but I was simply being with him in such a way that my full attention was focused upon him rather than some of that attention being concerned with my own behaviour. When the session ended I felt an acute embarrassment: I did not see how I could come out of that very intimate meeting and begin to dissect the experience with the observers. The observers' views were interesting: while many had grasped the intimacy of the meeting and noted how my 'presence' had helped Terry to go very deeply into his experiencing, some of the observers saw me as relatively 'motionless', very 'quiet' and even some-what 'detached'. These observations were so different from the experience which Terry and I had had that at first we could not under-stand them. However, when we watched the video ourselves, we saw exactly what these observers meant. Apart from one point in the session when I moved from sitting opposite Terry to sit alongside him, I was virtually motionless throughout the 40 minutes. I also said very little: only about 5 per cent of the total speech was mine. Furthermore, it was easy to see how I could look 'detached' although nothing could have been further from the truth: my body posture did not give the normal signals of one who is attentively listening; instead of sitting at the edge of my seat maintaining a solid eye contact with Terry, I would at times sit back or fold my arms or look into the same space in front of us. It was amazing to watch the video taken by a camera at distance and see the different picture it gave from how it had actually *felt* in the session. For most of the session I had been sitting alongside Terry, as close as one can be to a person without physically touching him. I could feel his body with my own, sense every movement of feeling that was going on inside him without *knowing* precisely what that feeling was or to what it related. As he talked about earlier experiences I felt close enough to him to be able to presume that my sensing of those experiences was close to his own, such that I could comment on the sense of his experi-ence as if I was experiencing it myself. In the session I was also aware that I did not need to *do* anything with my body or with my speech to show Terry that I was with him: I knew I was with him, but more important than that, I knew that *he knew* I was with him. This degree of mutuality, where the counsellor and client understand each other across different levels of perspective, is characteristic of a meeting at relational depth.

I believe that the counsellor's *understanding* of the client is much over-emphasised in counselling. Most of the time it is not important that the counsellor understands what the client is relating. Indeed, a trap for the person-centred counsellor is to be deflected away from being close to the experiencing of the client and drawn into trying to understand what the client is saying. Usually this has the result of pulling the client out of his experience in an effort to explain it to the counsellor! Much more facilitative to the client's movement into his experiencing is to be as close to that experiencing as possible.

An oft-quoted maxim about person-centred counselling is that the essence of the person-centred approach is more about *being* than about *doing*. This is never more relevant than when we consider the counsellor meeting the client at relational depth. The power of the experience for the client is that someone has been present with him in parts of his world where he has huge fear; the fearless presence of the other gives enormous support. In a commentary added to the video some months later, Terry reflected upon the power of the experience for him:

> All the way through the session I was filled with such a wide range of emotions – it felt like I was exploding. Watching that on the video, it doesn't really come across. Another thing was that it felt like Dave was doing an enormous amount right through the session. Again, when watching the video he seems to be very quiet and there were a lot of silences. But 'silences' isn't a word that I would use. It felt like – at points it was unbearable, the amount of emotion and the intensity of the interaction between the two of us.

Carl Rogers devoted only about one and a half pages to the quality he called 'presence' in an article published shortly before his death (Rogers, 1986). He referred to the experience in a somewhat mystical fashion, but as always, his words communicate very effectively:

> When I am at my best, as a group facilitator or a therapist, I discover another characteristic. I find that when I am closest to my inner, intuitive self, when I am somehow in touch with the unknown in me, when perhaps I am in a slightly altered state of consciousness in the relationship, then whatever I do seems to be full of healing. Then simply my *presence* is releasing and helpful. There is nothing I can do to force this experience, but when I can relax and be close to the transcendental core of me, then I may behave in strange and impulsive ways in the relationship, ways which I cannot justify rationally, which have nothing to do with my thought processes. But these strange behaviors turn out to be *right* in some odd way. At those moments it seems that my inner spirit has reached out and touched the inner spirit of the other. (Rogers, 1986: 199)

If Rogers and I are talking about the same experience then I would suggest that it might be referred to in mystical language or in terms of existing concepts, whichever is the writer's preference. I suspect that we could go a long way towards describing this phenomenon by considering it as a combination of two circumstances. First, there is a blending together of high degrees of the three core conditions of empathy, unconditional positive regard and congruence. In conceptual terms these three concepts come close together when we look at their extremes, particularly empathy and congruence (see Mearns and Thorne, 1999: chapter 5). The second circumstance is that the counsellor is able to be truly *still* within herself, allowing her person fully to resonate with the client's experiencing. In a sense, the counsellor has allowed her person to step right into the client's experiencing without needing to do anything to establish her separateness. This second circumstance is made much easier for the counsellor if she is not self-conscious. In Section 12 of this book Brian Thorne gives a beautiful account of how the counsellor can tune herself for that unself-conscious way of relating.

It is easy to say that the pre-requisites of offering the client a meeting at relational depth are an unselfconscious 'stillness' and a coming together of the therapeutic conditions in high degree. But, to the beginning counsellor this feels like a huge, unattainable objective, particularly if we add the expectation that the person-centred counsellor should be able to offer that depth of engagement to every single client who walks through her door, no matter the degree and nature of that client's self-protections. That is the objective of professional development in person-centred counselling: not only to be able to offer this depth of engagement to the warm, friendly, accepting client – but equally to the client who has developed ways of being which are so unattractive (see Mearns and Thorne, 1999: chapter 4) that they are generally effective in keeping other people away. It is important that the new counsellor does not expect too much of herself at the beginning – this is a developmental process that may involve an array of self-development objectives as well as several hundred hours of counselling practice (see chapter 2, 'Meeting the client at relational depth' in *Person-Centred Counselling Training*, Mearns, 1997a for more detail on that development process).

Working at relational depth with clients blows the myth, largely held by practitioners from other therapeutic disciplines, that person-centred counselling is simply a superficial 'supportive' approach to counselling suitable only for articulate clients whose difficulties are not too profound. Case illustrations of 'Bobby' and 'Alexander' in *Person-Centred*

Therapy Today (Mearns and Thorne, 2000) show the detail of working at relational depth with two difficult but very different clients. Another published example is the severely withdrawn, traumatised war veteran 'Bob', in chapter 5 of *Person-Centred Counselling in Action* (Mearns and Thorne, 1999). Although the client was entirely mute, the passage describes a powerful experience of the depth of contact between him and his counsellor (p.100). Indeed, it is interesting to reflect upon the importance of the counsellor's engagement at relational depth in work with clients who are profoundly 'detached' in terms of communication. Often the only meaningful thing that we can do as a counsellor is to be *with* such a client, staying as close to his experiencing as possible, even when we do not understand the context or even the content of that experiencing.

The quote which follows comes from a client who had gone through a period of frequent psychotic episodes during which the counsellor had maintained contact. The client tries to describe his experience of the counsellor during those times. Perhaps he is describing a client's view of relational depth even though normal, superficial communication was blocked.

> I could see her there, but I couldn't *say* anything. I wanted to tell her that I could see her there, but I couldn't tell her – it was scary – maybe it was like having a stroke and being paralysed so that I could *feel* her but I couldn't tell her. She must have understood me, because she never asked me any questions – you can't answer people's questions when you are like that. She would say some things – things which went along with what was going on in me, things like ... well, I don't remember any particular things – but I do know that she was close – she was close *inside* me.

KEY POINT The professional person-centred counsellor can offer the client – any client – a meeting at relational depth. While that affords enormous potential to be able to work even with people whose disturbance is profound, it begs many questions of the counsellor's development.

3 What is involved in offering wider contracts to clients?

Philip and Michelle

The following presents the thoughts of the person-centred counsellor, Philip, about his work with the client, Michelle.

Visiting a client in the middle of the night is not a common occurrence, but sometimes it is necessary. This was to be my third session with Michelle in the last 24 hours. While I was physically tired I was content that this crisis work was an important part of the therapeutic process. Working with clients once a week is sufficient for most, but when a client is in desperate crisis that pattern of attention is simply not enough. In a once-a-week session with a client much of the content is *second-hand* in the sense that the issues and crises of the past week are being relayed and perhaps replayed. However, this current work with Michelle is almost totally in the present – the issues she is facing are alive during our contact. That contact consists of at least a one hour session every day but there are also occasions such as this when she is reaching the peak of her personal crisis and I need to give more time.

As I walk towards her bed I do not smile in a reassuring 'doctor-like' way because my role is not to take her out of her pain but to be in it with her. I sit down beside her bed, take her hand and stroke it gently. After a minute or so I say 'Where are you, Michelle?'

In Box 3.1 the person-centred counsellor, Philip, presents some of his thoughts about his work with the client, Michelle. Counselling practitioners would vary dramatically in their judgements of Philip's work with Michelle. Some would define Philip as '*over-involved*' with Michelle, simply on the grounds of his willingness to extend the boundaries of their normal sessions, regardless of any other factors. Other practitioners might look with some suspicion at Philip's holding and stroking of Michelle's hand, not to mention the idea of visiting a client in the vicinity of her bed!

Within the person-centred approach practitioners also recognise the notion of 'over-involvement', but judgements of that kind are not made on the basis of simplistic *structural* factors such as the timing of sessions, mild physical contact and the physical location of the work. If the profession made judgements of work in simple structural terms then some of the best examples of 'successes' would have to be re-categorised, for example Barnes and Berke (1991) and Thorne (1987). If a counsellor's work is to be judged in structural terms then the understandable reaction is for the counsellor to become more detached and self-protective in relation to her clients. However, in the person-centred approach the exact opposite is required of the practitioner: the invitation of the approach is that the counsellor becomes as fully involved as possible with her clients, without being emotionally over-involved. This requirement of full involvement is critical where the counsellor is working with clients whose difficulty is particularly acute or chronic. Such clients require a therapeutic space which offers as much containment as the prison they have built around themselves.

It is important that person-centred counsellors who are choosing to work with more demanding clientele and more involving therapeutic contracts are able to be flexible in the way they work while ensuring that they are in full control of the work. Structural aspects of the work like frequency of sessions, length of sessions, the possibility of crisis 'call-outs' and working in settings that are safe for the client rather than familiar for the counsellor, are all factors which may be varied by the experienced and well-supported counsellor. One of the problems with this suggestion of entering into wider contracts with clients is that it is sometimes the most inexperienced and inappropriate practitioners who are attracted to working in this way. Inexperienced workers should rigorously avoid engaging in such wider contracts because the danger is that these would be sustained by the needs rather than by the professionalism of the counsellor.

A counsellor embarking on such work must be supported by her ongoing *supervision*. Person-centred counsellors who are offering wider contract work with clients require more supervisory support as a matter of policy. Furthermore, that supervision needs to be flexible in its response to the worker. Rather than wait a week for the next supervision session, the counsellor may need some more immediate attention after particularly intensive working. In therapeutic work which demands daily working with profoundly disturbed clients, supervision may also have to be offered daily.

Counsellors who are working with clients in wider contracts should also be aware of the *social context* of that work. Although counselling essentially involves the practitioner and the client, in fact there are numerous other people connected to the social system of counselling. Many different sets of expectations impinge upon the counsellor and client as they engage in their seemingly private activity. These may include the expectations of friends and relatives of the client, the counsellor's employer, professional colleagues of the counsellor and even the close relatives of the counsellor. Although these other persons do not determine the nature of the counselling, it is potentially dangerous for the counsellor to go out on a limb with a client without regard to these members of the social system.

The importance of attending to the social context and the expectations therein might best be illustrated by reflecting back to Philip's report in Box 3.1. The reader might look at this extract once again and consider whether the social context of the work makes a difference. For example, does it matter that Philip was working with Michelle in a hospital setting rather than at her home?

> **KEY POINT**   Counselling does not need to be restricted by structural conventions which dictate the length, frequency, location and nature of the process; indeed some clients cannot feel safe unless a wider contract is offered. However, working with wider contracts carries the obvious danger of over-involvement and is not for the inexperienced practitioner.

4 Extend the core conditions to the whole of your client – introducing 'configurations' of self

The person-centred discipline of attending to the client as a 'whole' person is sometimes misunderstood as implying that the person-centred counsellor should relate to the *wholeness* of the client and should not attend to the elements and dynamics within the personality. If a person-centred counsellor worked from that misconception she would learn that it reduced her ability to work at depth with many clients. That especially applies to the client for whom the forces within his self have effectively cancelled each other out, where, for example, the influence of the actualising tendency has been countermanded by an integrated system of introjected restrictions. To work with the 'whole' of this client would require us to be attentive to the voices of all the different aspects of the client, endeavouring to extend the therapeutic conditions to all of them.

Box 4.1 is contributed by a client (Mearns, 1993b). It illustrates the conflict which had raged within her personality for many years. The client referred to the main players in this conflict as 'the nun' and 'the little girl'. A crucial point to note about the work with this client is that at no stage did the person-centred counsellor push for the separation of these aspects of the personality, nor did the counsellor offer labels to the client for these different parts. The importance of this strict policy is explained in Section 20 of this book.

Box 4. 1

The nun and the little girl

Elizabeth survived into her early 40s before her life began to disintegrate. That disintegration could be traced back to her survival and adaptation to some powerful conditions of worth in childhood. These conditions of worth included the following:

- You are good if you are caring
- You are not good if you express dissent
- Crying for yourself is selfish
- You are evil if you hurt your mother
- You are evil if you hurt your father
- Your value is in the service you give to others
- Second best is failure

Elizabeth survived these conditions of worth and lived a meaningful life, at least in other people's terms. It was a surprise to all who knew her when she broke down during the early stages of counselling training. She had previously worked for several years as a counsellor in a voluntary organisation but her new training quite quickly reached the fragile aspects of her personality. She left training and went into therapy where she gradually uncovered competing dimensions of her personality which she referred to as 'the nun' and 'the little girl'. These two main parts of her personality can be characterised by the following quotes from the therapy tapes:

Part A: 'the nun'	Part B: 'the little girl'
I am a caring person	I don't really care
I love my clients	I really despise most of my clients
I don't do enough as a person	I despise myself
I love my husband dearly	I despise my husband
I cry for the pain in the world	I am a sham
I don't know why you bother with the likes of me	I am going to leave the whole damned lot of them (her family)
I am always letting people down	I am so, so scared

Continued

I do *try* to do the right thing   Help me to get out
I'm just not good enough   Don't desert me
If only I could get rid of that   Help me destroy that
    bad little girl inside me   pompous nun

During the breakdown of the fragile balance held between these aspects of her personality, a third, unnamed, aspect developed. This part can be characterised by other quotes:

Part C

I am really struggling with all of this
I am getting so tired ... so very tired
I don't know whether I'm going to make it
I am crying for *me* nowadays
Sometimes I look at myself and it is like watching a boxing
    match going on inside me
This depression feels totally different from before. It feels much
    blacker and I feel fully *in* it rather than fighting it

Although she experienced considerable pain in relation to this third aspect of her personality, it did represent a force towards integration.

Rogers' Self Theory is useful for understanding the dynamics within Elizabeth's personality. The part which she describes as 'the nun' appears largely to be composed of *introjected* aspects of her self structure (see Rogers, 1951: 498, Proposition 10). This largely introjected part of her self helped her to survive the conditions of worth under which she had lived, but that part contrasted sharply with 'the little girl' who had largely been *denied* (see Rogers, 1951: 503, Proposition 11). There was no place for 'the little girl' in Elizabeth's normal life and yet this dimension of her self had struggled to survive within Elizabeth's experience of herself.

The dynamic illustrated in the case of Elizabeth is fairly common with an introjected 'good' aspect of the self and another, presumed 'bad', aspect which contains the ghosts of the denied aspects of self. This second aspect has never had a chance to discover how far it is 'good' or not: the only way it has been able to survive is by maintaining a position of opposition to the other part of the self. It is worth noting that Elizabeth was by no means suffering from Dissociative Identity Disorder ('multiple personality'). Much nonsense is produced nowadays under the label 'Dissociative Identity Disorder', usually by counsellors who are not schooled in psychopathology. Elizabeth simply found it conceptually convenient to ascribe labels for the *conflict* within her experience of her self.

In working with a client who has a pluralist conception of his self, the person-centred counsellor's task is to manifest the therapeutic conditions in relation to *all* the aspects of the self. This is what is meant by working with the whole person. It is absolutely critical that the counsellor *values* each of these aspects of the client's personality, *listens* to each of them carefully and is *congruent* in her relationship with all of them. A common error in counsellors who are not sufficiently well trained is to align more strongly with one part of the personality against the other. The danger in this naive procedure is that the counsellor is actually colluding with part of the client to reject another important part of himself. At the very least this tends to block or elongate the therapeutic process.

It takes some discipline on the part of the person-centred counsellor to offer the therapeutic conditions to *both* parts of the self and to resist the exclusive invitations of the different aspects of self because each can put up a strong case for the vilification of the other. For example, in counselling Elizabeth there were phases when 'the little girl' was in open revolution against 'the nun' and other times when what was happening was more like a counter-revolution. During these different phases each aspect of the client's self invited the therapist to reject the other (for example: 'Help me destroy that pompous nun').

It is useful for the counsellor to remember that *all* the aspects of the client's self will have been important in survival. Although Elizabeth may currently despise 'the nun', the construction of that part of her self would have been important for her survival within her family. Indeed, it is difficult to imagine how the young person could have survived those oppressive conditions of worth laid down for her without the help of 'the nun'. The 'little girl' may be despised and feared by 'the nun' because she is potentially disruptive if not destructive to Elizabeth's early life. And yet, the survival of the 'little girl', albeit in the unvoiced underlife of Elizabeth, carries the potential for Elizabeth to become more than a role-playing caricature.

Working with the intra-self dynamics of a client is very much like working with a family. In person-centred work with a family the counsellor would be concerned to communicate the therapeutic conditions to all family members present. She would also be wary of being perceived to align more strongly with one member than the other. In the course of work with a family the person-centred practitioner would endeavour to help each person to hear the other through the empathy offered by the counsellor. All this happens in work with different parts of a single client's self. As the work proceeds each part will begin, however tentatively, to feel sufficiently valued to allow itself to listen to the other parts as they are expressed in communication with the counsellor. This opens the door to the client empathising with the different parts of his self and leads to the client seeing the importance which each part has played in his survival. Thus begins the process towards self-acceptance.

The first edition of this book (Mearns, 1994) contained the first published presentation of this pluralist conception of the self after it was introduced in a public lecture (Mearns, 1993b). Since this time the term 'configurations' has been coined to denote 'parts' of the self (Mearns, 1999). The term 'configuration' was adopted when it became evident that these parts are highly sophisticated. Their early function might have been to provide a home for a specific introjection or denied aspect of self, but thereafter they can assimilate numerous other elements to expand their functioning and to develop more fully their self-protective and expressive functions. The word 'part' (though it is the term clients tend to use) seemed too small for this sophisticated phenomenon that had developed its own internal and external dynamics and which would even 'reconfigure' itself to serve its function more adaptively. The psychology of configurations and configuration dynamics is detailed elsewhere (Mearns, 1999; Mearns and Thorne, 2000; Mearns, 2002a, b and c; Cooper, 1999).

It is important to maintain a client-centred discipline when working in this area. Some clients symbolise their self in pluralist terms and others do not. The person-centred therapist does not insert a pluralist conception when that has not come from the client – always the discipline is to 'stay close to the client's symbolisation' whatever that may be. Our configurations within self, if that is the way we see our self, represents a delicate area of discovery which is extremely vulnerable to any suggestions from the counsellor. There is no more striking example of the effects of such counsellor invasion than the client in Section 20 of this book who says: 'I have an "Abused Child" inside me . . . I think it belongs to my previous therapist'.

> **KEY POINT** Working with the 'whole' client may mean offering the core conditions to all the aspects of the client even when these aspects are in conflict and mutually rejecting.

5 Don't get 'hooked on growth'

Person-centred counsellors are attuned to the matter of personal growth. They are skilled in hearing even a small 'growthful' voice in their client and encouraging its fuller expression. Yet, it is fascinating to analyse supervisees' audio-tapes of counselling sessions, frequently to discover that other voices expressing an opposite 'not for growth' imperative are often ignored, de-emphasised or not even heard. The challenge for the person-centred counsellor is to offer just as strong a therapeutic relationship to these apparently resistant or negative aspects.

Growth is not a unitary phenomenon – rather, it involves a process of balancing opposite forces and gradually reconfiguring that balance. The *process* of growth includes both a forward moving pressure to elaborate, diversify and seek more stimulation, and also a restraining influence which cautions against a pace of movement that can risk security. Our car is moved more skilfully if we can have access to both the throttle and the brakes – both are part of the moving process. This 'dialectical' process whereby a balance is achieved by the action of opposite forces is common in nature, for it offers a more sophisticated 'dual control' system. Even within our body, 'homeostasis' is generally obtained by dual control mechanisms, for example, the secretion of two hormones with opposite effects.

There was a period in Carl Rogers' work, at the height of his popularity when he moved to California in 1963, when a more simplistic 'unitary' conception of growth became established. Obvious movement in an apparently 'growthful' direction was lauded and 'not for growth' voices were vilified (Mearns and Thorne, 2000: chapter 9). It is easy to see how this perception could develop. Many clients presented with a growth process that appeared restricted, often by the excessive restraining influence of conditions of worth. The growth process had not progressed and the symptoms of that were dissatisfaction and depression. Not surprisingly, the awareness gained in counselling released pent up movement in obviously 'growthful' directions. That kind of experience masks the fact that growth is a dialectical phenomenon controlled by opposite vectors. Indeed, we can sometimes see that in our client sometime after the release of that pent-up movement – their movement slows and they begin even to come back a little – paying more attention to voices of restraint within them. The pendulum has swung beyond its point of balance and needs to make a correction. When clients make major decisions during that initial release, it can be difficult for them later.

If we are to relate fully with our client in his growth process, we need to attend to *all* the aspects of his experience – the voices that push for movement and also those which urge caution, because they are both parts of the growth process. Person-centred counsellors often have a developed sensitivity for the obviously growthful parts and have to develop an equal sensitivity to those parts of the client's system that appear to reflect the opposite vector. Remembering that both vectors are part of the same growth system can help the counsellor to attune her ear. Can she hear and value equally, the parts of her client which are saying, 'Perhaps I should stop now', 'I just want my life back the way it was – even though it wasn't great', 'I'm too tired to go ahead with it'. Also, this vector is sometimes expressed in a more self-punishing fashion: 'What makes me think I can change anyway!', 'Basically, I'm pathetic – I'll never be able to change things', 'I don't know why you bother with the likes of me'. Even more challenging for the counsellor is the client whose expression is punitive but directed towards the counsellor: 'You're not much of a counsellor, are you!', 'I'm obviously wasting my time coming to see you', 'My mother says that I've got to stop seeing you because you are putting a lot of fancy ideas into my head'.

Even learning about these various representations of the 'not for growth' vector does not equip the counsellor with the knowledge to be competent. The reality is that we can only ever know the meaning of a 'voice' through the client himself. An expression cannot be defined by the counsellor as 'growthful' or 'not for growth' – it needs to be understood in terms of the client's unique system. One client cuts his wrists as a way of 'punishing' himself for seeking to change and another client cuts his wrists as a 'punishment' for his intransigence. We cannot understand our client's growth dynamics by interpreting his behaviour or statements – we need to hear from him what everything means.

In any case, the challenge for the counsellor is the same: to listen to *all* the parts of her client, as was emphasised in the previous section. In that fashion they will all be heard – the whole 'family' of parts will be involved in the therapy process. The dialogue between Charles and his counsellor illustrates aspects of this process:

Charles has arrived a little late for the session. He greets the counsellor in an offhand manner and slumps down in his seat. The counsellor begins in her usual fashion.

Counsellor: Is there anything you want to begin with today?

Charles: Not really – everything's going fine.

Counsellor: You don't look as bright as you usually do.

Charles: I'm OK – really.

[*Counsellor leaves the silence*]

Charles: Why don't you say something?

Counsellor: I'm stuck with knowing what to say. I was going to say, 'Fine, what should we start with today then?'. Then I thought, 'But we've started already – Charles has come in, sat down – he looks different from most days and he has said he is OK. I was struggling to know what to say. I guess I was concerned for you, but I didn't know if you wanted that concern right now . . .

[*Silence*]

Charles: Every time I come along the street to your office a voice within me screams 'STOP – DON'T GO IN'. When I didn't come two weeks ago, it wasn't because I had forgotten, like I said – it was because a part of me deliberately wanted to stand you up – it wanted to think of you waiting for me. Even now, as I speak, another voice is calling me names.

Counsellor: What names?

Charles: 'Patsy', 'Fool', 'Idiot', 'Crawler' . . .

Counsellor: I'd like to meet this other part of you as well – do you think that would be possible?

Charles: He is sneering at you.

Counsellor: What is he feeling?

Charles: Scorn . . . anger . . . and . . .

Counsellor: And?

Charles: . . . Fear

Counsellor: . . . This is a scary place for him . . .?

Charles: . . . This is not a place for him – he doesn't want me to be here.

Counsellor: . . . He feels it's not safe for you to be here?

Charles: I get upset when I come here. I feel sad about me and my life. I want to change things when I'm here.

Counsellor: And he doesn't want you to get upset, feel sad about your life and want to change things . . . think I understand that – I think I understand him being scared for you.

Charles: It's *so* scary. What if I can't *really* change things – I'll feel worse than ever. Why don't I just forget it . . .

[*Silence*]

[*Charles cries. The Counsellor kneels beside him and puts a gentle hand on his shoulder*]

[*Later*]

Counsellor: A part of you wants to change things and a part of you is scared of what you might lose if you try to do that. Those parts *both* seem important to me.

In this extract Charles is able to express a part of him which is resistant to the process that is happening to him. He feels 'scorn' and 'anger', but underlying these is his 'fear'. This is a normal aspect of the growth process even though it seems to work in the 'wrong' direction. It is important that there is space for it in the counselling room because if it went unheard it could exert its influence in other ways.

The counsellor helps the process in a number of ways. Firstly, her silence after Charles' 'I'm OK – really' is better than simply moving on. She does not know how to respond to this different 'arrival' of Charles, but she does not ignore it. Secondly, she meets Charles' challenge to 'say something' by saying absolutely *everything* which she is experiencing in relation to the event. A fully congruent response such as this is powerful in many ways. It shows her concern and it also trusts the client by laying her communication fully open. The part of Charles which is resistant has been heard and is being honoured. This helps him to give it a voice, even though the material is difficult. Thereafter the counsellor continues to be open to meeting this 'other part' despite the fact that it is disparaging towards her. When the 'fear' is reached the counsellor appears to understand its quality which leads to Charles' important symbolisation: 'It's *so* scary. What if I can't really change things – I'll feel worse than ever. Why don't I just forget it. ...' Charles, in all his aspects, has been well heard in this counselling session.

> **KEYPOINT**   The growth process includes opposite vectors representing forward movement and restraint. The challenge for the person-centred counsellor is to extend the therapeutic conditions to all aspects of the process in the client.

II

The Development of the Counsellor

6 Counsellor 'paralysis': diagnosis and treatment

Box 6.1

Counsellor 'paralysis'

This client, recently separated from his wife, has been harbouring the hope that she will return to the marriage. However, the day before this session she has told him that she has filed for divorce.

Client: So, I suppose there's nothing I can do about things, eh? [*Looks at counsellor*]

Counsellor: [*Silence*]

Client: I mean, basically the decision is not up to me, it's up to her, isn't it?

Counsellor: Yes, I suppose it is.

Client: [*Silence*]

Counsellor: What else is difficult for you?

Client: Isn't this thing big enough?

Counsellor: Oh yes, I didn't mean ... I mean, it is very difficult for you – I can see that.

Client: Yes.

This trainee counsellor is not functioning. For whatever reason, she is unable to respond with even partial empathy. In any realm of human endeavour potentially skilful practitioners can on occasion become so blocked that they fail to exhibit even basic skills.

It is not uncommon for counselling trainees to experience episodes of 'paralysis' like that which is illustrated in Box 6.1. When the counsellor is in a paralysed condition she is under stress and is so aware of her own behaviour and its possible implications that she cannot perform even the simplest task of responding. Similar phenomena are found in other areas of skilful behaviour where chronic or prolonged stress can induce a complete breakdown in the flow of performance: the professional golfer finds that she has lost her nerve with short putts; the skilled tennis player cannot throw the ball up for the serve; and the good student experiences dramatic examination paralysis.

In some other counselling approaches paralysis may be masked by the trainee introducing some form of exercise or activity which is usually ineffective since it has not been selected under the mediation of the counsellor's empathic sensitivity to the client. In person-centred work, the trainee has no such illusory escapes from paralysis and is painfully exposed to its symptoms such as:

1. *The counsellor fails to respond to her own silence.* In the normal course of human dialogue silences are usually *owned* in the sense that the conventions of human communication would dictate which party should normally break that silence. For example, if the client clearly finishes his statement and looks directly at the counsellor, the conventions of communication would normally lead the counsellor to respond. However, where counsellor paralysis exists the practitioner may not be able to observe or respond to these cues. In Box 6.1 the counsellor's silence in response to the client's first statement is an example of this symptom.

2. *The counsellor gives inappropriately brief responses to client questions or statements.* Sometimes a brief response is appropriate and helps the client to focus, but when the client has given considerable detail on a difficult issue and the counsellor merely responds with 'Yes', 'Oh', 'I see' or 'Mmhm', they have, in effect, not responded to the client.

3. *The counsellor responds with a partially empathic 'closer'.* While even partial empathy usually tends to encourage the client's further and deeper exploration, where the empathic response is delivered without any implied question, but more as a conclusion, the result is usually to close the exploration, for example: 'Yes, I can see that that was difficult', 'No, you couldn't have done that', 'That was the only decision you could make'. The counsellor's second response in Box 6.1 'Yes, I suppose it is' is an example of a partially empathic closer.

4. *The counsellor shows an inability to 'track' the client.* A basic skill in person-centred counselling is getting on to the client's 'track' (Rennie,

1984; 1998) and continuing the empathic flow of that track. However, when the counsellor is paralysed her functioning becomes so disjointed and incoherent that the ability to track the client is lost. An example of this is given in Box 6.1 where the counsellor completely fails to follow the client's track in relation to his feeling of powerlessness over his wife's decision. Instead of following through on this track the counsellor says 'What else is difficult for you?' Most often this symptom takes the form of the counsellor asking the client a wholly inappropriate question, as in this example.

5. *The counsellor shows an increased willingness to adopt a parental, advice-giving or nurturing role.* A sign of regression in a counsellor's behaviour is to slip into simplistic attempts to give the client something concrete like guidance, advice or practical help instead of working therapeutically with the client. While this can be an effect of counsellor paralysis, if it is maintained over a period of time it could be symptomatic of a deeper problem in the therapeutic relationship or indicative of a counsellor who has failed to develop therapeutic ways of working.

6. *The counsellor accelerates the ending of the work.* When clients are uncomfortable with a counsellor they sometimes escape by means of a sudden 'flight into health'. This has the effect of winning freedom from the counsellor while allowing both parties to save face. There is a parallel form of this for the counsellor who is experiencing discomforting paralysis. She may find herself selectively emphasising the client's achievements, strengths and successes while simultaneously playing down the client's continuing difficulties. Counsellors who are skilful in this ineffectiveness may even manage to turn continuing difficulties into achievements: 'Yes, it is still very painful for you, but look how you have managed to keep going despite it.' If the client accepts the hint, he terminates counselling while the counsellor can still preserve her illusion of effectiveness.

Ineffectual functioning as is illustrated in Box 6.1 may arise from the counsellor's lack of training but it may also indicate a temporary paralysis brought about by stress. The otherwise effective counselling trainee may begin to experience stress induced paralysis fairly early in training. The trainee feels the pressure of trying to do everything *right*. In person-centred work the trainee quickly develops a superficial understanding of the therapeutic conditions and believes that she will be a better counsellor if only she can consistently display behaviours in line with these therapeutic conditions. Hence, she becomes the warm, accepting and empathic counsellor overnight and falls into the habit of continual checking and censoring of responses which do not fit the 'accepting empathic' mould. Responses are censored if they might sound too strident, impatient, demanding, interpretative, judgemental, trivialising, cold, superficial or too directive! With every possible response being monitored and judged critically in this way it is not surprising that the trainee counsellor falls into response paralysis: there appears to be no way of responding because every response might violate some guideline or other. Indeed, the supreme 'Catch 22' is that by over-monitoring these responses the trainee feels that she has denied herself the possibility of being spontaneously congruent, so even a response which passed the earlier monitoring procedure might now be deemed 'wrong'. The trainee might further tie herself in knots by questioning the *motives* underlying her responses to clients. When faced with the attitudinal demands of the therapeutic conditions it is both natural and common for self-doubt to rear its paralysing head.

The task of the trainer (see Mearns, 1997a) in relation to trainee paralysis is to endeavour to reduce the pressure the student is experiencing. Trainers might emphasise that counselling training is a developmental process with work on self and the growth of skills going hand in hand. Trying to force or 'portray' the therapeutic conditions, rather than nurturing their gradual development, is not merely a pointless process, but one which is likely to arrest the counsellor's natural development. Ideally a training course might develop norms which appreciate and even celebrate the trainee's relative lack of skill in the early stages. Indeed, the making of 'mistakes' might even be *encouraged* with the training period being regarded as a time when one can afford oneself the opportunity to be a learner who gets things wrong. Certainly, the training period is a much better time to get things wrong because there is a network of considerable support. Trainers also need to be 'expansive' in their feedback to trainees. Constantly 'picking over' the student's utterances to point out how these could be improved feeds into an obsessiveness with detail and could encourage paralysis. Alternatively, trainers might emphasise that there are '500 roads to success' in any counselling interview and the important dimension is the quality of the 'contact' which is made with the client. If the 'contact' is good the technical detail of the counsellor's responses becomes less important – if, for example, she is 'missing' the client empathically, the client will likely help her out. A more expansive approach to feedback on the part of the trainer will get away from the 'shoulds', 'should nots', 'musts' and 'must nots' that can feed the student's paralysis. For example, recently I worked with a group of students who had got hold of the idea that person-centred counsellors should not ask questions. Of course, this was utterly paralysing – any time they found their response to a client was being framed as a question in their mind they had to censor it.

I assured them that I asked a lot of questions in counselling sessions. I also pointed out that an empathic response was an implicit question. Perhaps this myth had arisen from a specific instance where the question had been directing the client out of his experience rather than staying in it, like the 'What else is difficult for you?' in Box 6.1. It is not the fact that an intervention is phrased as a question that is important. What is important is where it is coming from in the trainee – is it grounded in her tracking of the client or is it derived from her *lack* of contact with him?

It is easy to give intellectual credibility to an argument which suggests that training should be a developmental process but it is difficult to establish that in the minds of trainees who are educated within a culture that emphasises success rather than development. It is difficult for trainees to put themselves into the role of 'learner' or 'apprentice' (Mearns and Thorne, 2000: 126), initially expecting little of themselves but looking to develop over time. Instead, people tend to put pressure on themselves not to 'fail' in front of others. There is nothing so paralysing of skill than a fear of failure.

> **KEY POINT**   Trainee counsellors are particularly prone to stress-related 'paralysis'. The solution lies in regarding the training period as a time to experiment and to develop rather than feeling one has to get it 'right' from the outset.

7 Beware the need to appear 'clever'

Counsellors are often attracted to the person-centred approach for the right reason: that it offers a method of counselling which keeps the client at the centre of events, emphasising the counsellor's task as one of creating a relational safety and intensity that helps the client to increase his awareness and re-engage his energy for living. Although counselling in this way is a highly skilful activity, it does not give much opportunity for the counsellor who has a strong need to be seen as 'clever'. Those counsellors who have that need from the outset would find more latitude in other approaches that emphasise the directive qualities and interpretative abilities of the counsellor.

The need to appear clever may become a hazard for the person-centred counsellor as she develops. The notion of being a 'facilitator' can be attractive to counsellors early in their professional development because it does not demand that they behave like the expert which they do not feel. However, as the counsellor becomes more confident in her work with clients, merely facilitating the release of the client's power may become less satisfying for the person who needs to feel that she is more at the centre of events.

This degeneration of the person-centred counsellor into an 'expert' may be furthered by the under-estimated difficulty of maintaining the personal, emotional challenge of person-centred work. The approach emphasises the quality of the counsellor's *being* with the client rather than what the counsellor *does* with the client. Maintaining a fully involved way of being over years of professional practice is much more demanding than developing a repertoire of things to *do* with the client.

The result of these factors may be a person-centred counsellor who gradually becomes more concerned with doing than being. She may find herself offering more interpretations, unexamined intuitions, quasi-theoretical constructions and creative bits and pieces which are thrown into a soup that tastes new and interesting for the practitioner but runs the risk of drawing more power to the counsellor. Tony Merry offers a well-written account of the ways in which some person-centred practitioners endeavour to justify anything as person-centred (Merry, 1990).

It may be difficult for the counsellor to track the impact of her pseudo-cleverness on the client because such ways of being attract expert power to the counsellor and may silence the client in the relationship. Box 7.1 reproduces a few client complaints never expressed to the counsellors under criticism.

Box 7.1

Some clients' views of their counsellor's cleverness

- She asked me to do some weird things – like sit in silence because I was talking so much and needed to slow down. She was right, but it felt uncomfortable – I didn't know when it was OK to start speaking again.

Continued

- She said I was blocked and we should do some painting to release it. I hate painting but I went along with her. I hated every minute of it but I couldn't tell her.
- He kept looking for ways to 'get my anger out'. Eventually he succeeded – it came out. He looked so self-satisfied that I wondered who I had been angry *for*. I felt a little dirty at that moment.

It is difficult to find a solution to this problem for person-centred practitioners: even with good supervision the emotional demands of a person-centred way of working are enormously difficult to sustain over time (see Section 8). However, there is available one potentially large resource for the counsellor who needs to *feel* clever rather than necessarily to express it. Person-centred counselling carries with it a wealth of theory, some of which has been examined in research but still more which can be hypothesised and explored in the future. Within the self theory and theory of therapy underpinning the person-centred approach there is a potentially enormous resource for the counsellor to feel 'clever' in translating these into work with the client in order to create a large therapeutic space for the client and also to understand the changing processes within the client. For studious person-centred counsellors this body of theory can be an enduring source of intellectual and creative satisfaction. Perhaps what distinguishes the well-trained person-centred counsellor is the willingness to study the underlying theory and weave that into her work. Exactly that is found on training courses for supervisors (Lambers, 2000). Re-entering training after some years of experience finds the practitioner hungry to develop the cognitive aspect to supplement their affective learning. Sometimes it is astonishing to see counsellors who, in their initial training, had been diligent in their avoidance of theory suddenly blossom into theoreticians during supervision training.

KEY POINT The game of 'Look how clever I am' is a fairly natural aspect of human relating. However, the person-centred practitioner is asked to play it in private or in relation to colleagues, but not with her clients.

8 'Burn-out' and how to avoid it

'Burn-out' is a much used term in present-day society. Indeed, the concept has become so ubiquitous that it is rarely defined. Figuratively the term is a good one: when a worker becomes 'burned-out' it is as though the flame which had provided her drive and energy for the work has slowly become extinguished either through lack of fuel provided from within or by the suffocating effect of a reduction of oxygen in her environment. Burn-out is commonly regarded as a consequence of excessive or prolonged stress: not the kind of stress that puts us under pressure to act vigorously and quickly but the kind of stress which results from a prolonged negative balance between what we are putting into the work and what we are getting out.

This 'economic' metaphor is fitting because it also extends to the behaviour of the worker in the process of burning out. During that degenerative period there are two broad categories of 'symptoms' of burning-out. These correspond, first, to the efforts the counsellor makes to *reduce her investments* in the work and, secondly, to her attempts to *inflate the dividend* she receives from the work. Let us consider each of these categories of burnout symptoms in turn.

First, what does it mean when the person-centred counsellor 'reduces her investments' in the work? As with any degenerative condition, we should look for not just one 'symptom' but a cluster of changes, all of which suggest that the person-centred counsellor has begun a process of minimising her investments in the work. The first symptom is likely to be a gradual reduction in the person-centred counsellor's therapeutic use of *congruence*. Indeed, gradual burn-out is a particular problem for workers in the person-centred approach *because* of this immediate effect on congruence which is one of the central tools of the person-centred counsellor's work. The 'congruent use of self' requires freshness, openness, a clarity of self-perception and a willingness to explore unknown territory in the therapeutic relationship. All these attributes suffer when the worker is experiencing the stress that leads to burn-out.

Becoming more *impatient* with clients and getting *tired* more easily in the work may also be symptoms of burn-out when occurring alongside a reduction in congruence and other factors. There can, of course, be numerous other reasons for impatience and tiredness. A more reliable symptom of the counsellor's burnout is that she becomes less attentive to the *individuality* of the client: the counsellor becomes more problem-centred than client-centred. A problem-centred approach allows the counsellor to set in motion a 'treatment plan' which relates to the characteristics of the problem. This can offer the worker a much less demanding process than having to treat each new client as an individual with a unique experience of the problem.

Another interesting symptom of impending burn-out can be the person-centred counsellor's increasing *rigidity* in contract setting. This is not to say that the person-centred counsellor should be flexible to the point of being sloppy in contract setting because it is important for clients to feel the solidity of a clear contract. However, when the person-centred counsellor is beginning to withdraw in order to reduce burn-out stress she may become unnecessarily limited and rigid in the contract, giving little flexibility in the scheduling of sessions. Whereas at an earlier time of working the counsellor might have extended the safety net she offered the client by giving her home telephone number for use in times of crisis, that extension to the contract is no longer offered. In ways such as these the counsellor becomes more rigid.

These possible symptoms of burn-out should be part of supervisor training in the person-centred approach because it is the supervisor who is in the best position to perceive the early signs of the counsellor withdrawing self or limiting the demands on self within the work. As with most stress effects the person under stress is slower to become aware of or acknowledge the process than an external person such as the supervisor. Supervisors should feel a responsibility to voice concern about symptoms such as those mentioned above.

The 'economic' metaphor mentioned at the beginning of this section suggested that another way in which the person-centred counsellor could attempt to improve the balance was to enhance the value of what she was getting out of the activity of counselling. Later in this section we shall look at some of the ways in which the counsellor may realistically add value to her work experience, but first we should be aware of the fact that this side of the equation may be enhanced in an artificial or illusory fashion by the counsellor under stress. Whereas the counsellor's gradual withdrawal of the self from the work might be described as a movement

in the direction of *under-involvement,* in this second category the counsellor is erring in the direction of *over-involvement.* This over-involvement
may take the form of the person-centred counsellor coming to define
herself as the powerful agent in the client's change. Rather than seeing
herself as a quiet facilitator of the client's empowerment, the counsellor
begins to regard herself as the architect of her clients' future existence: in
extreme cases the counsellor might come to ascribe quite unreal power to
herself. Any supervisor who heard statements like those which follow
would be concerned that this was a counsellor who was approaching
burn-out.

- I feel that I can see right through my clients to the true heart of them;
- I have never felt the power of my healing so strongly;
- My intuition has developed to an extraordinary degree – I know what
  my client is going to say before he says it;
- I just *know* that I can help him if I am given the chance.

These statements reek of the kind of self-deception which may accom-
pany prolonged stress in a work context that can suffer from not being
sufficiently open to public perception. The tyranny which can result is
aided by the fact that some clients would readily wish to give up their own
power in the face of the mystical/magical power of such a counsellor.

While it is difficult enough for a supervisor to challenge the growing
under-involvement of a counsellor, it is more difficult to confront over-
involvement because the counsellor has a great need to hold on to the
dividend which is yielded by such illusions.

A good discipline for the person-centred counsellor is to address the
question of burn-out at regular intervals in supervision, even though no
suspicion has arisen. One way of doing this is to review the balance and
nature of investments and returns: to question what the counsellor is
investing in the work and what she is getting out of it. In making this
analysis it is important to recognise that the counsellor must obtain
return from the work, but that the nature of that return should be open
to investigation.

Avoiding burn-out involves finding ways in which the dividend for the
counsellor can be maintained throughout her working life. Some of the
following possibilities may be relevant to different counsellors.

It is important for a worker to feel *stretched* in order to make gains
from the work in terms of self-esteem. That 'stretching' can be brought
about by altering either the *intensity* or the *variety* of the work experience. If a counsellor is working day after day at a level which does not
demand a great intensity, then that may be difficult to sustain. However,

if some of the work is more demanding either in terms of the severity of the client's difficulty or the intensity of the therapeutic contract, then the counsellor is more likely to feel the benefits of the stretching which results.

Introducing *variety* into the work is as important as varying the intensity. That variety may be in terms of the range of clients and their difficulties, but it can also be achieved by involvement in activities other than counselling. In order to achieve a work balance which is nourishing, many person-centred counsellors do not counsel full-time. Even if their major emphasis is counselling practice, they would often include activities such as group work, training and research as part of their overall workload. Not only do these other activities introduce variety into the working life but they are all potentially stimulating of each other.

Person-centred counsellors might wonder at the suggestion that they could be involved as *researchers* but that possibility certainly exists to a much wider extent than is generally accepted. Every time the person-centred counsellor is embarking on a new therapeutic relationship, she is engaging in the activity called 'research'. In that work she will be examining a number of research questions: how far can the self theory underlying the person-centred approach describe this client's existence? In what ways are the therapeutic conditions being manifested in this relationship? How does this individual therapeutic process compare with person-centred theory on therapeutic process? What is the client's experience of this work? How is this work affecting me as a counsellor? The counsellor works at the leading edge of human experiencing: the possibilities of being stimulated by seeking understanding of the human condition are available as one further alternative to drifting into burn-out. One of the most accessible and expert authors in this area of 'practitioner research' is Professor John McLeod. As well as producing key writing on the subject (McLeod, 1994; 1997; 1999; 2001), McLeod edits the largest circulation 'practitioner research' journal worldwide (BACP, 2002).

Much more could be written about the ways in which counselling may be linked with related activities in order to create an overall balance of work that maintains and stimulates itself. The creation of this balance is a more effective way of preventing burn-out than, for example, taking regular time away from counselling. Although a 'rest' period may be essential in the case of the counsellor for whom burn-out has reached an advanced stage, it is not in itself a cure for burn-out – it simply takes the person temporarily away from the unequal balance. A more effective, longer-term, approach would be to address that unequal balance and find ways of improving it for the counsellor.

In this chapter we have focused on just a few examples of how the balance may be improved by altering the intensity and variety of the work. It should be noted, however, that this question of balance needs to be approached in relation to the counsellor as an *individual*. Indeed, increasing the 'dividend' for any counsellor can only really happen if it is examined in relation to that counsellor's central constructs, values and indeed to her individual spirituality.

> **KEY POINT**   The 'economic' balance between what the counsellor is *investing* in the work and the dividend she is receiving from it offers a useful structure through which the counsellor, assisted by her supervisor, can monitor the risk of 'burn-out'.

9 Personal therapy is not enough

The experience of being in therapy as a client is useful to the person-centred counsellor because it gives her an opportunity to appreciate the *role* of the client and, in particular, how it can feel to be in that less powerful position. This can help the counsellor to become aware of some of the difficulties the client may experience in terms of forming a therapeutic alliance with the therapist. If the therapy experience is long term, it may also help the counsellor to realise how easy it is for the therapeutic relationship to become stultified and the importance of the therapist's congruence in maintaining the health of the relationship. At times it is also important for the counselling trainee to engage in private therapy during training in order to give more attention to personal issues which have emerged.

While these are important reasons for counsellors in training to seek experience of the client role, it should not be presumed that personal therapy substantially meets the *personal development needs* of the counsellor in training. It is an easy step for trainers to set a requirement for personal therapy and presume that this will go a long way towards serving the trainee's personal development needs, but that assumption should be challenged in the case of person-centred training. A central difficulty lies in the fact that personal therapy tends to have a much narrower focus than the personal development which is required in person-centred training. Personal therapy attends to the issues which are of foremost personal importance to the client, for example, the therapy might be principally concerned with the negotiation of a major life transition or it may be concerned with the client's most intimate relationships. Either of these issues could dominate a lengthy period in therapy. While this experience would help the trainee counsellor to learn about some aspects of self which would have wider applications in terms of her work as a counsellor, the range of issues and conflicts which the therapy considered would not adequately cover the personal development needs in person-centred counselling training (see Mearns, 1997a: 98–99 for a list of 25 generic personal development needs).

It is important to introduce a more *public* perception of the personal development needs of the trainee. If left to individual therapy the issues which will dominate will be those which are introduced by the client: areas about which the client is blind cannot receive attention unless they manifest themselves in the relationship with the therapist and are then deemed by the client to be important. In counsellor training many vital areas of personal development are brought to the surface in trainees who have been through considerable experience as a client in therapy without the issues ever arising. One example is the trainee who discovered such rigid ethnocentric attitudes that it was completely impossible for him to work with clients outwith his own class and race. This was such a pervasive problem that it threatened to terminate his training and yet no hint of it had surfaced in three years of prior and current therapy. Similar was the male trainee who found that he could relate perfectly adequately with women at a superficial level but was deeply misogynistic at more intimate levels of relating. Once again, this had never emerged in his lengthy period of therapy with a male therapist. Another trainee became rigidly ego syntonic when put under the slightest threat or criticism in relationship. In other words, he found it totally impossible to empathise in such circumstances and was only able to understand the client in terms of his (the counsellor's) own experience. This had emerged in relation to his previous therapist but it was never seen as central to his difficulties and did not receive sustained attention. Needless to say this difficulty surfaced quickly in personal development groups during training as did the entrenched difficulty of another trainee who engaged well with people until there was a high emotional content of any kind, at which point he would 'blank out' and retreat into what he later called his 'black hole'. The feedback which this latter student received from other students in a training context quickly raised and addressed this important concern but, to his knowledge, it had never arisen in his two years of therapy.

Personal development for professional working is so crucial to the person-centred approach that it cannot be left to the vagaries of individual therapy. This is one reason why person-centred counselling training by distance learning, even with concurrent personal therapy, is such a nonsensical proposition that it does not merit consideration.

Experiential groups of different kinds are powerful sources of personal development learning and work. The experience of 200 hours of experiential groups is much preferred to 200 hours of personal therapy because the public perception of the trainee becomes part of the agenda as well as issues which are raised by the trainee herself. It is customary for professional training courses in person-centred counselling to work with a variety of different kinds of experiential groups and, indeed, to introduce the norm of openness and confrontation into the whole working of the training to such an extent that trainees feel a responsibility to face each other with difficulties which may pertain to their personal development.

Before personal therapy is entirely dismissed, it should be said that there can be a place in training for therapy which is specifically designed as *training therapy*. Training therapy would exist explicitly to address the personal development issues being raised in the various experiential groups of the training course. There would be an argument for the training therapy being more closely monitored by the training course than is normally the case with personal therapy (see Mearns, 1997b for a fuller discussion of 'training therapy').

There is danger of a growing norm in counselling which presumes that personal therapy will meet personal development needs for counsellor training. Other counselling approaches will make their own decisions on this but personal development is too central an issue in person-centred training for it largely to be pushed to the periphery.

KEY POINT   Do not presume that the personal development needs of a person-centred counsellor are substantially met by prior or concurrent personal therapy.

10 What to do if you are not perfect

The person-centred counsellor is someone who has gone a fair way down the road of understanding her own personality dynamics. While this development will have been sufficient to help the counsellor to become more self-accepting and open to others, it is unlikely that she will be an entirely conflict-free human being. However, we can hope that she is aware of residual unresolved conflicts and is able to work around them.

For years I have seen trainees give themselves such a hard time over the personality conflicts which they have uncovered during training. Often the trainee makes her task impossible by imagining that each personal conflict which surfaces must be surmounted and worked through or she will not be able to become a good counsellor. Sometimes these personality conflicts then become so feared that the trainee finds it difficult to deal with them openly in the training contexts which are explicitly designed to help her to work with such difficulties.

Perhaps the problem with perfection is cultural. Human beings in so-called Western culture have a tendency to think in terms of extremes, probably as a result of being reared under the simplistic notions of Aristotelian logic which cannot cope with the concurrent existence of opposites. The result is that 'ideals' are seen in terms of extremes – usually unattainable extremes at that. Hence, our counsellor will tend to presume that she must continually work in the direction of resolving all her conflicts before she can become a better counsellor.

My suggestion is that while the counsellor will indeed be able to resolve and dissipate the power of some personality conflicts, others will not so easily be resolved and may have to be *managed* in the sense that the counsellor develops systems for controlling or working around these conflicts during counselling. Two quite different examples might illustrate this emphasis on developing awareness and control rather than waiting for resolution of personality conflicts.

'Thelma' discovered that her main personal difficulty as a new counsellor lay in the area which we might broadly describe as 'spirituality' (in her case, mixed with religiosity). Thelma referred to this area as one which held a 'fatal attraction' for her in her work with clients. She would narrow on that aspect of the client's experiencing and become seriously over-involved because it contained many potent but also confused and unresolved issues for her personally. Yet, during her training period, and helped by her trainers and fellow course members, she developed considerable skills as a counsellor. She addressed the issue of her spirituality in various dimensions of her training, but her development could progress without waiting for resolution simply by being aware of the pitfalls and helping her to exercise *control*. In the counselling opportunities which ran alongside her training she intentionally chose to work with clients who had different backgrounds from herself and whose spirituality was experienced and expressed in quite different fashions, hence reducing the likelihood of her identification and projection. Also, she developed the control that when coming to spiritual dimensions in her client she would maintain a very strict way of working, concentrating exclusively on partial or accurate empathy so as to ensure that she followed rather than led the client. In collaboration with her supervisors she actually put a 'ban' on herself attempting any 'additive empathy' when touching the area of her client's spirituality. In this way Thelma worked effectively around her difficulty while still exploring that in other parts of the training experience. She was able to progress as a counsellor and she also developed management skills which she would be able to employ later in her counselling career over other difficulties which might arise.

'Patrick' had worked therapeutically with children for many years before entering counselling training. While his work with children had met with widespread acclaim, it was a considerable challenge for Patrick to work with adults where his deep-seated feeling of inferiority made him doubt his actions and generally disempowered him. Far from avoiding that area of difficulty during training, Patrick was able to use the training context as one which would provide considerable scope for his support and learning. As well as mapping out the difficulty and exploring its roots, Patrick was also able to monitor his counselling practice quite closely, using audiotapes which he would review in supervision soon after sessions. The thing which he repeatedly discovered was that he could actually function well as a counsellor in relation to his adult clients but that he tended to misperceive and under-value his interventions. The practice of repeatedly testing his perceptions against those of his supervisors and supervision group helped him to map out the actual ways in which his misperceiving operated. In this way

Patrick was able to continue his training despite the fact that the underlying personality conflicts were slow to resolve. The progress he made in the actual counselling practice contributed in a positive way to his self-esteem and gradual self-concept change. He extended his training period by two years but completed it to his own satisfaction.

If Thelma and Patrick had felt the need to resolve their underlying personality conflicts before continuing with their counselling training then they might never have got back to that training. As it was, they not only developed their skills as counsellors, but learned very important personal management skills around mapping the effects of personal difficulties and developing control in relation to those difficulties. Both of these counsellors made good use of the broad support which is available during the training period.

In this section we have emphasised that while personal development is a crucial aspect of counsellor training, we should note that it is perfectly possible for counsellors to forego the attainment of perfection in personal development terms and learn the skills involved in working around areas of difficulty. For my part, I am somewhat suspicious of counsellors who seek perfection in personal development terms and prefer, as in the case of my own counsellor, someone who is a trifle imperfect (see Box 10.1).

Box 10.1

My counsellor

My counsellor is a moderately screwed-up individual. He has a deep-seated *passion* which I find attractive, though that passion has no particular focus, or at least it has had many foci over the years. As is usually the case, a person's strength is often also his weakness and my counsellor is aware of the ways in which his passion can raise for him the dangers of emotional over-involvement. My counsellor also gets moderately depressed at times, though he seems able to work despite that. At these times I suspect he operates at about 75 per cent of maximum, holding 25 per cent back to keep himself safe (and keeping me safe in the process). At these times I find 75 per cent of him to be plenty for me to use in a facilitating way. I suspect my counsellor's psychopathological leaning is in the direction of a

Continued

mild personality disorder (indeed, we have talked about that). His difficulty is not so great that he cannot empathise or that he is seriously ego syntonic, but it is enough to make him susceptible to projection at times. But, again, he is aware of that tendency in himself and can easily repossess his projections and not continue to push them upon me. My counsellor can laugh at himself which tells me that there is some degree of self-acceptance: I believe that this self-acceptance is important for both of us. For me, he is a good counsellor – a man that I can trust to be whatever he is, without pretence. He does not seek to usurp my power, nor to impose his own. He does not need me to think of him as 'clever' or 'wise' nor any such foolish thing. I like his passion and his humour: indeed, I love him dearly.

KEY POINT Counsellors do not need to have resolved all their personality conflicts – some of these conflicts can be made safe through awareness and management.

11 Using the large unstructured group to develop congruence in person-centred training

Congruence is generally accepted as the most difficult of the therapeutic conditions to develop. Early in the counsellor's development there is a tendency to *portray* an empathic and accepting way of being (see Section 6). As development continues there is a need for the person-centred counsellor to break through this inclination towards portrayal of empathy and unconditional positive regard so that when the counsellor chooses to relate in this way, for example in a counselling setting, the endeavour will be wholly congruent. This attention to the development of congruence and the forsaking of mere portrayal of empathy and unconditional positive regard is one of the features that distinguishes advanced person-centred training from the more superficial variety, which regards empathy and unconditional positive regard simply at the level of skill development.

One of the major opportunities for the development of congruence in advanced person-centred counselling training is the use of the large unstructured group meeting, sometimes called the *community meeting* (see Mearns, 1997a: chapter 10 for a fuller account). This group may contain anything from 20 to 40 people and is comprised of all the trainees of the course and some or all of the core staff. The meetings are unstructured in the sense that there is no agenda except that which is raised by the participants.

Such large group meetings can be helpful to any course or working group of people as a forum for airing and dealing with difficulties as these arise. In that sense they have a function in maintaining the 'health' of the community. However, if such large group meetings are to have a function in relation to the counsellor's development of congruence they must be regular, frequent and take place over a fair period of time. For example, on a one-year full-time person-centred training course there is likely to be at least one community meeting per week lasting between one and two hours. Part-time training might have a small amount of community time each day or a larger block every few meetings. The function of the large group as a forum for congruence development is generally slower to develop in part-time training because members are more tied to the incongruence of daily living and, understandably, find it difficult to experiment with more congruent ways of relating during community meetings, which represent a relatively small portion of their lives. This difficulty in establishing the large group as an important activity in the eyes of trainees is one of the main differences between full-time and day-release training.

The large group meeting is not an easy experience (Sturdevant, 1994). Participants, in general, prefer smaller groups because trust and safety are established more quickly. It is for this very reason that the large group carries enormous potential for the participant's development in relation to congruence, though that opportunity depends on the participant's will-ingness to take it. In small groups the participant can more easily develop ways of being that are accepted by the other members of the group. The large group is valuable because it is more difficult for people to settle into a safe yet satisfying way of relating. It is not easy to establish trust quickly because there is a greater variety of people and more conflict of needs. A simple *portrayal* of empathic and accepting ways of being can be effective in establishing and maintaining trust in small groups but the number and variety of people in the large group leads to this being challenged more surely and quickly than in smaller groups. While that challenging of norms as they become established can make the experience more uncomfortable for participants, it also affords the opportunity to experience interpersonal relationships on a fairly intense level without reliance on safe and constrained ways of relating. As the life of the large group continues there is more 'free meeting' among participants, that is to say, there is more meeting where the individuals are communicating their experience of each other simply and directly without pretence or defence. While there would be a tendency in the earlier stages to hide behind more defensive ways of communicating, the members gradually realise that they not only have less need to do this, but that that way of communicating is essentially frustrating and self-defeating. As the community meeting evolves in this way participants see and feel the difference between congruent engaging with each other and the previous, more guarded ways of relating. They experience the quality of unconditional positive regard and empathy where these are being offered *congruently* rather than offered by means of a more polite, self-protective portrayal. They also experience the freedom and power felt by both people in congruent communication. That experience is very *releasing* for the participant – here she is beginning to *trust her own process* rather than attempt to survive on her superficial *portrayal* of empathy and unconditional positive regard. In this way the development of congruence encourages and is encouraged by the growth of self-acceptance.

This *release into congruence* enhances both the quality and the quantity of the counsellor's unconditional positive regard and empathy. At earlier times in the counsellor's development there might have been an underlying fear which could be represented by the words: 'I do not *know* if I am really the kind of person who can be accepting and empathic with people so I had better *try* really hard to portray empathy and unconditional positive regard.' The result of that effort to portray the conditions is an incongruent and thereby hollow empathy and unconditional positive regard. However, later in the development of congruence, the counsellor has discovered that this fear is dispelled: she knows that the qualities of unconditional positive regard and empathy can flow congruently from within her rather than needing to be forced. The beautiful paradox in this is that counsellors invariably report that they are now able to *release* their empathy and acceptance more fully and in relation to a broader range of clients. This dynamic is quite common in human experience: when we no longer feel forced to *portray* a way of being we are then able to *be* that way more easily. Interestingly, but not surprisingly, this finding that counsellor empathy and unconditional positive regard are enhanced by the development of congruence reflects Rogers' eighteenth proposition:

> When the individual perceives and accepts into one consistent and integrated system all his sensory and visceral experiences, then he is necessarily more understanding of others and is more accepting of others as separate individuals. (Rogers, 1951: 520)

KEY POINT The development of congruence requires the trainee counsellor to forsake the tendency to 'portray' acceptable ways of being and to begin to risk being themselves. Paradoxically, the large experiential group, by its demanding nature, can offer a vibrant opportunity for the counsellor's awareness and also experimentation with her congruence.

---

12 Developing a spiritual discipline

BRIAN THORNE

'I am compelled to believe that I, like many others, have underestimated the importance of this mystical spiritual dimension' (Rogers, 1980: 130).

Among the 'post-Rogerians' a battle has raged for some years about the importance of Rogers' claims in the final decade of his life to have discovered a new and powerful dimension in the therapeutic relationship. In short, he believed that when he was functioning at his best and therefore offering the core conditions with maximum effectiveness, something qualitatively different could happen. He described this as the experience of discovering that simply his *presence* was releasing and helpful. 'At those moments', he wrote, 'it seems that my inner spirit has reached out and touched the inner spirit of the other. Our relationship transcends itself and becomes a part of something larger. Profound growth and healing and energy are present' (Rogers, 1980: 129). In the face of these startling assertions many person-centred practitioners tend to be embarrassed or even dismissive. There are certainly those who state, either publicly or privately, that such wildly grandiose claims are attributable to Rogers' declining faculties or to a kind of *'folie de grandeur'* which sometimes afflicts great men as they approach death.

I find myself in a different and growing camp from these detractors. Unlike them I am excited by Rogers' attempt to articulate his experience of the mystical. When he speaks of the 'transcendental core' of his being I find no conflict between this concept and the notion of the 'actualising tendency' which underpins the person-centred understanding of personality and therapeutic process. My ready endorsement of Rogers' claims springs from my own experience of precisely the phenomena which he describes. What is more, I believe that, as a person-centred counsellor, I have a responsibility to attend to my own being and to the relationship with my clients in such a way that this quality of presence with its remarkable capacity for promoting growth, healing and energy is more likely to be experienced. Clearly, as Rogers himself states, nothing can be done to *force* such an outcome within the course of a therapeutic encounter and the thought of setting out deliberately and consciously to create the experience of presence is preposterous. The issue is more subtle and complex: it involves the willingness of the therapist to live out consistently and profoundly the philosophy which the person-centred approach embraces. More particularly it requires what I have come to call the disciplined practices of self-exploration and self-acceptance and of the focused holding of the absent client. It is my belief – and experience – that a commitment to such a discipline on the part of the counsellor greatly increases the likelihood of therapeutic relationships where the transcendental core of client and counsellor can be brought together with a resulting release of healing energy.

In my own life the practice of self-exploration and self-acceptance comprises a number of different elements and I shall discuss these briefly in a moment. I am sure, however, that each practitioner must discover for himself or herself the practice with which he or she feels most comfortable. There can be no blueprint which is universally applicable. It goes without saying, too, that the discipline I am describing supplements and greatly extends the benefits of the traditional supervision relationship but in no way replaces it. The discipline I have worked out for myself has five elements and involves a consideration of my current response to various aspects of my experiencing. The task in each case is to conduct an exploration and to arrive, if at all possible, at a position where I am able to accept myself for what I am. The discipline lends itself to a variety of settings – to periods alone in my study, to the walk home after a long day in the counselling room, to a journey by train. What matters for me is that it should be done systematically and regularly. The first element concerns my relationship with my body. I reflect on my thoughts and feelings about my physical being and try to face those areas where I am self-rejecting or self-deprecatory. I attempt to be as compassionately disposed towards my body as possible and ask myself how I am treating it through what I eat and drink, through the clothes I wear, through the rest I give it and the activities I pursue. Where it seems I am lacking in compassion I resolve to become more caring of the body which has the awesome task of carrying me through the world. The second element concerns my relationship with others and here I deliberately exclude my clients (they have their turn later!). I ask myself how cherished I feel and how cherishing in turn I am to others. Sometimes I discover that I am making do on starvation rations. I am not putting myself in the way of love and appreciation and I am even failing to smile at the postman. Self-acceptance is scarcely nurtured by such closedness and I want to open myself again to loving and being loved. The third element focuses on my use of time. I ask myself what I am doing in my work and with my leisure. Whatever I discover I am resolved to move to a position where I can feel as acceptant as possible of the time structures in which I find myself and of the activities to which I am committed. The fourth element concerns my awareness of the created order of which I am a part. By this I do not mean simply the natural environment of trees, flowers, animals, sun and rain but also the creations of humankind: buildings, works of art, music, poetry, beauty in all its forms. Reflection on this element sometimes reduces me to tears when I am forced to acknowledge that I have not read a poem for a month or allowed my eyes to linger on a tree all week. Such deprivation is a sign of self-neglect rather than self-acceptance. Finally, and most important of all, I put myself in the presence of my God. If I were an atheist or a humanist I would, I suspect, give myself over to the meaning of my life or to whatever higher power or influence irradiated my destiny. This is an exercise in total surrender so that I am immersed in God and allow myself to experience my unique and absolute value without hindrance or self-recrimination.

The discipline I have so far described has as its sole objective the cultivation and the maintenance of a loving disposition towards myself. The self-acceptance of the person-centred counsellor is a necessary cornerstone of person-centred practice and it is my contention that a discipline of this kind, regularly and systematically practised, leads to an enduring self-love which releases the counsellor from all self-preoccupation and greatly increases the possibility of a transcendental encounter with clients which is powerfully healing and releasing. There is, however, a second practice which, I believe, further increases the likelihood of such an encounter and this I call *holding the absent client*.

Many clients complain that they find it difficult to believe that their counsellors care about or even think about them between sessions. For some, the sense of abandonment and the agony of separation are weekly occurrences. Clearly, however, it is unhealthy for any counsellor to become so preoccupied with a client that his or her own inner life becomes disrupted by such concern. Nonetheless, in my experience, it is powerfully enhancing of the relationship if the counsellor holds his or her clients in mind on a daily basis. The discipline is simple: it consists of focusing on each client in turn, bringing him or her to mind and calling up a visual image of the person in question. The counsellor then holds the client in a metaphorical embrace of acceptance and understanding for a minute or two. I am convinced that such a discipline greatly strengthens the relationship between counsellor and client and taps into those very forces which become so powerfully operative in the transcendental encounter. The client need never know of the counsellor's daily discipline on his or her behalf although there are those who are profoundly aided by such knowledge of their counsellor's commitment to them.

In the last year of his life Carl Rogers gave a remarkable interview to Michèle Baldwin on the use of the self in therapy (Baldwin, 2000: 29–38). In expansive mood, he returned to the theme of what it is through experience and training that enables a counsellor to be fully and courageously present to a client. He describes himself in this interview as 'too religious to be religious' and it is clear that in this somewhat ironical statement he is pointing again to the underlying spiritual dimension in the therapeutic relationship. In similar fashion, my own work has increasingly brought me to the conclusion that a spiritual discipline is not an optional extra for the person-centred practitioner but a vital aspect of his or her personal and professional commitment to a way of being and working which extends far beyond the confines of the counselling room (Thorne, 2002).

> **KEY POINT**   Rogers' late reference to the spiritual dimension in person-centred counselling deserves serious attention. The counsellor has a responsibility to develop a spiritual discipline which will enhance the quality of presence which he or she brings not only to the therapeutic relationship but to every aspect of his or her life.

III

The Therapeutic Alliance

13 You do not need to be an 'expert' on the client group or issue to work expertly with the client

> It has been nice to have been treated as a woman rather than '*a sexually abused woman*'. You have been willing to hear how my life is for me rather than making assumptions. You have even allowed me to explore my positive experiences in relation to the incest rather than my previous counsellor who made me feel worse about myself for having those feelings. She seemed to presume that those positive feelings were simply further evidence of my oppression and would soon be replaced by anger. When that didn't happen she said that I wasn't '*ready*' for counselling. She knew a lot about sexual abuse, but not much about me.

This client's evaluation of her two counselling experiences reminds the person-centred counsellor of the importance of centring the work in the experience of the client rather than in terms of other people's experience of the client issue.

Within counselling circles there is a growing norm which suggests that working with particular client groups or specific client issues requires prior training in the culture of that group or issue. In just the same way as the medical profession categorises patients there appears to be a superficial logic about doing the same in counselling. However, the current state of the medical profession is that it treats 'conditions' rather than people and there is a danger that counselling may go down the same road. There is now a proliferation of training courses and also books on a host of client groups and issues, including race, age, disability, gender, sexual orientation, the bereaved, the dying, anorexia, depression, anxiety, suicide, ME, addiction, trauma, HIV and AIDS. All of the research underpinning specialist theory in these areas is of potential value to the person-centred counsellor, but it is important to know how this theory can be used in such a way as to maintain the fundamental person-centred orientation rather than working in a fashion which stereotypes the client.

In learning how to use theory on client groups and client issues, the first important step is to realise that this body of knowledge tells the counsellor precisely *nothing* about her client. In the social sciences theoretical knowledge gleaned from an averaging of human experience is not predictive of the experience of any one person. For example, it is not uncommon for victims of sexual abuse to go through a time of feeling inappropriate guilt. While this may be observed in a fair number of cases, it does not mean that our abused client *will* experience that guilt, so the counsellor should be wary of expecting that or of searching for it. Rather than apply this piece of theory to predict her client's experience, the person-centred counsellor would do better to listen carefully to her client's actual experience. It can be difficult for the counsellor to *manage* the riches of her theoretical knowledge about client groups or issues. In the endeavour of tracking the actual experience of the individual client, that body of theoretical knowledge may serve as *misinformation* if the person-centred counsellor allows it to interfere with her empathy.

Although such bodies of knowledge and theory may not be as predictively useful as we might wish, they can still support the counsellor in three important ways. First, a study of the human experience of different client groups and issues can help to broaden the counsellor's experience, albeit vicariously. The effect of this on the counsellor's personal development should be to make her more open to a variety of human experience. A second crucial function served by studying different client groups and problems is as part of addressing prejudice. One of the critical paradoxes in the therapy domain is that prejudice is anti-therapeutic and most counsellors carry prejudices. That statement is not intended to be controversial; it is simply a matter of fact. A large part of the self-development agenda (see chapter 7 in Mearns, 1997a) concerns the discovering and challenging of prejudices. One dimension of this is to give ourselves wide exposure to literature on the group that is the object of the prejudice. Prejudice is fed by a lack of knowledge and knowledge begins to weaken prejudice. For example, there is a wealth of fascinating literature on gay, lesbian and bisexual experiences as well as some key 'guiding' texts for the practitioner (Davies and Neal 1996, 2000; Neal and Davies, 2000). A third important function of such theoretical knowledge is the added security which it offers the counsellor: in particular, it offers the counsellor ways of understanding observed client behaviour which might otherwise have been confusing or frightening. For example, in working with war veterans as a client group, it is not uncommon to find that the experience of being in war was simultaneously the most horrific event in the person's life and also the moment at which he felt most alive. This phenomenon can be most disturbing for some veterans who cannot understand it and feel guilty about the 'buzz' they experienced, not to mention the fact that they would like to seek out the experience once again. Veterans who experience this effect are often slow to speak of it with others lest it meets with a response of confusion or judgement which they themselves already feel. It can be helpful for the counsellor to be aware of this phenomenon, not because it helps her to *predict* the experience of her client, but so that she is not confused or shocked if a client should present it. For example, the heterosexual counsellor who has learned about institutionalised homophobia and how alienating that can feel for gay, lesbian and bisexual clients, will have adjusted her practice to eliminate heterosexist assumptions. For example, she will not assume that her client's partner is of the opposite sex. It is not merely 'politically correct' to make those adjustments – it is a matter of social inclusion.

The challenge, then, to the person-centred counsellor is to use knowledge of client groups or issues not to *predict* the behaviour of an individual client but to help her widen her experience so that she can understand that behaviour once it is presented. No matter how much knowledge the person-centred counsellor may have of the client group or issue the starting point is always the same: an endeavour to understand how this individual client experiences his or her world.

> **KEY POINT** Knowledge and theory about specific client groups and client issues is *not* a prerequisite for person-centred work with clients from those groups or with those concerns. Such knowledge is not predictive of the client's experience, though it can considerably aid the counsellor's understanding of the client's experience.

14 Be 'beside' the client but not 'on the side of' the client

Box 14.1

Letter from a client's wife

Dear

I wanted you to know that you have destroyed a family. When Jim [her husband] first went to see you I was delighted. I had been pushing him to do that for years. But all that happened was that he became alienated from me and has now deserted all of us. Not once did you consult me and even when I telephoned you to ask for a meeting you let Jim know about it and you refused.

I have long been a supporter of counselling but I thought that a counsellor would be more caring for a family.

Yours sincerely,

The writer of the letter in Box 14.1 presumes that the counsellor has influenced her husband to leave the family. Whatever the realities for the other people involved, it is easy to see how this woman could presume that the counsellor had taken sides with her husband against her.

It is a common presumption that the person-centred counsellor is 'on the side of' the client: indeed, even some people who are peripherally involved in counselling might see the role as one of taking the side of the client and 'supporting' him in that way. However, that is both a naive and dangerous conception about the role of the counsellor: the counsellor is not there to be a support in the sense of someone who will share the weight of the client's life and decisions. Instead, the counsellor is there to create a context where the client can explore all his thoughts and feelings, integrating past events and future aspirations into his understanding of present behaviour.

The person-centred counsellor will want to be 'beside' the client rather than being 'on the side of' the client. The counsellor will want to be as close to the experiencing of the client as possible, showing an understanding of that experiencing and helping him to shift from side to side to see other facets. However, being beside the client in this way is quite different from being on the client's side.

There are two main dangers in the counsellor becoming over-involved and going over onto the client's side. The first is that if the counsellor has aligned with the client's orientation and decisions of today, what happens if the client reverses his position tomorrow? The counsellor's bias in being on the present side of the client might make it more difficult for the client to change his position even although that is what is dictated by his own process. This danger is particularly evident as we begin to understand more about the nature of 'configurations' within the self (see Section 4 in this book and chapters 6 and 7 in Mearns and Thorne, 2000).

A second reason for the person-centred counsellor to avoid over-involvement in this way is that the counsellor would be offering a form of support which she cannot be sure of sustaining. The counsellor would be sharing the weight of the client's life in a fashion which unrealistically lightened the load for the client in that moment. However, the counsellor who is on the client's side cannot guarantee that continued support. What does the counsellor do when the client, with the counsellor's support, leaves his wife, then returns to the counsellor to say 'Right, we've left her – what do we do now?' In lending this kind of biased support to the client, the danger is that the client makes decisions and carries out actions which he could not do without the added weight of the counsellor.

Becoming responsible in the client's life is a fairly common mistake made by less experienced counsellors in their desire to 'help' their clients. When the client defines 'help' as weight-sharing support then the counsellor may feel pressed to become over-involved. The dialogue which follows illustrates how difficult this issue can be in practice. This client has recently left her mother's home to live elsewhere after many years of attending to her mother's needs. She is feeling the strain of that decision and asks for more support from her counsellor.

Client: I don't feel that you are much *involved* with me.

Counsellor: How do you mean?

Client: Well, you just sit back there and are impassive to everything. I need you to be a stronger support to me. If I'm going to do this – if I'm going to survive this – I need *more* from you. I need you to be on my side, not sitting on the sidelines as you do. I get much more support from other women than I get from you – you're too detached.

Counsellor: I'm glad that you are getting that support from other women and I'm also uneasy about the fact that I've come over to you as 'detached' ... but I guess that I *have* been wanting to be 'on the sidelines' as far as the decisions you have been making. I want to help you to explore decisions but I don't want simply to narrow my support to particular decisions.

Client: That's all very well, but don't you see that I need your encouragement and your weight behind me and you telling me that I've done the right thing to leave her [her mother].

Counsellor: I *want* to be strongly here for you ... and I would want to be just as strongly here for you tomorrow if you told me that you were going back to your mother.

Client: That's not good enough. I'm doing a difficult thing – leaving her strengthens the pull on the elastic that pulls me back to her. If you don't give me more support I may be pulled back to her.

Counsellor: I'm sorry, but I can't give you *that* kind of support ... I feel quite split inside. Part of me wants to jump onto your side and put my shoulder behind you to support you. But the bigger part of me fears that I could be doing you an enormous disservice by taking sides in your life.

Client: That's not good enough for me. I need more support. Perhaps I'll look elsewhere.

KEY POINT The person-centred counsellor wants to be as close to her client as possible, but being 'by the client's side' is quite different from being 'on the client's side' which must be avoided at all costs.

15 Getting beyond 'transference'

Different therapeutic approaches have different emphases. For example, the understanding of 'empathy' within most psychodynamic work is fairly superficial compared with its meaning in person-centred work. In person-centred counselling empathy is a core concept involving a considerable depth of relationship and emotional engagement with the client. In empathy the counsellor is actually tuning into the client's experiencing process and gaining a sense of how it feels to be him. However, the notion of 'empathy' is much less central in most psychodynamic work and the concept itself is more superficial. Ute Binder (1998) uses the term 'cognitive social perspective taking' to denote this more superficial understanding of empathy as a process of imagining the view of the client.

In exactly the same fashion, 'transference', the tendency for the person to transfer feelings and reactions which were part of his earlier responses to parent figures onto authority figures (like counsellors) in his present life, is regarded as the fundamental concept within psychodynamic work. Indeed, the whole of classical psychoanalysis is built around transference which carries sophisticated meaning. In contrast, 'transference process' within person-centred thinking is regarded as an interference – a level of relating which is fairly superficial but which may need to be negotiated in order to sustain an engagement with the client at relational depth and so gain access to his 'existential process'.

Rogers (1951:114) took exactly the same view of transference as a dimension of relating which needed to be got through in order to meet the client more congruently. Other person-centred writers have been more overtly critical of the notion of transference. For example, in a paper entitled 'A counter-theory of transference' (1984) John Shlien argued that transference was largely manufactured by therapists in order to enhance their importance and help them to remain hidden. A lively debate provoked by Shlien's paper developed in the person-centred journals (Fischer, 1987; Kahn, 1987; Seeman, 1987; Strupp, 1987) and the consensus view seemed to be that transference phenomena do indeed exist independently of the therapist's encouragement but that it was debatable how important they were.

The person-centred counsellor will take great care not to encourage the development of transference. At best that would greatly elongate the therapeutic process and at worst it would further entrench the client's transferential relating. A salutary book which should be compulsory reading for anyone in the psychotherapeutic profession is *One to One* (1987) by Rosemary Dinnage. In this book the author interviews 20 clients who had been in therapy for an average of 12 years. Not only had the therapeutic process been grossly elongated in this way, but it was clear that they were still trapped in a transferential way of conceptualising their therapists. There must come a time when this type of process becomes challenged as 'transference abuse' (Heron, 1997).

The person-centred counsellor would try not to be a 'blank screen' upon which the client can readily project his or her transference-based expectations. The person-centred counsellor is a real person involved in a real relationship and being fully present within it. One of the important consequences of the person-centred counsellor's congruence is the way that it contributes to opening out and disentangling the transference which might otherwise take root in the relationship.

A useful way to look at the counsellor's congruence is that, in her communication with her client, she *shows her working*. The metaphor comes from school mathematics where the pupil is encouraged not just to give the answer, but to 'show her working' as well. So, the person-centred counsellor does not simply make powerful and mysterious pronouncements, but she gives all the detail of her processing. Compare the following counsellor statements made five minutes into a session where the client had arrived ten minutes late without saying why, and proceeded to be virtually silent for the whole five minutes, while apparently scowling at the counsellor:

1. I sense something's going on for you today.
2. I feel confused about our start today ... and uncertain about how to proceed. I want to ask you what's 'wrong' and I'm also hesitant – perhaps I've done something that I'm not aware of. I've sat on it for a few minutes, but I'm pretty curious ...

The first statement addresses the issue without disclosing anything about the counsellor's internal 'working'. It is a 'bold' statement, which puts all the onus onto the client and does not emphasise their 'relatedness' – that this is a shared endeavour where they will both take responsibility. If the client already feels vulnerable in relation to the counsellor, it is also a *powerful* statement. The vulnerable client could easily experience it as a 'pronouncement from on high'.

The second statement is slightly faltering – the counsellor is trying to give voice to *her whole process* in relation to this issue. She is not concerned to make it well-rounded, or particularly coherent – it is more important that it is a perfectly congruent expression of her whole process. The client might still have some strong feelings about the counsellor depending on what he is bringing to this session, but the counsellor's second response is less likely to compound and cloud the issue by further developing any transference which might exist.

Exactly the same discipline of 'showing our working' applies to the person-centred counsellor trainer in communication with trainees. Trainees can be expected to be less vulnerable to transference issues and to share more responsibility where those issues exist, but the trainer can help and can provide a good model by being transparent in her own dealings.

While the person-centred counsellor is concerned not to encourage the further development of transference she is equally attentive to working with it where it already exists for her client. She is alive to possible assumptions and projections the client might be making in relation to her and will confront these in order to work with them. Of course, that 'confronting' is done in the manner described above, with the counsellor 'showing her working'. Also, the person-centred counsellor will not presume that the issue is entirely a matter of the client's transference process – it could be that the counsellor has unwittingly fed into the process by behaving in a way which encouraged the transference. Hence, in the second statement earlier, the counsellor included: 'perhaps I've done something that I am not aware of'.

With a client who is particularly vulnerable to transference issues the person-centred counsellor will be inclined, regularly, to check on the experience the client is having of their relationship. Hence, checking on the 'unspoken relationship' (Sections 17 and 18) will become an important discipline because the client who is especially vulnerable to transference process may grossly misperceive the counsellor's communication. Margaret Warner (2002a) suggests that this difficult transference process may be a case of '*fragile process*' and this writer agrees. Sometimes there is a huge vulnerability in the client over transference issues. It is not simply that the client feels disappointed when others fail to live up to their 'transferred' expectations, but that their early parenting has led them to expect the worst from parent-like figures. They are caught in the fundamental existential conflict of, on the one hand the wish to be understood and prized and on the other hand, repeated experiences of being let down and put down when their need has been greatest. The transference phenomena encountered in relation to this client may be especially challenging for the counsellor. The client desperately wants the authenticity, prizing and understanding which appears to be offered, but if they risk opening themselves to it and once again it proves to be not real ... The counsellor needs both to understand this process and to be resolute in the consistency of what they have to offer. The reader is referred to Warner (2000) for a detailed account of fragile process.

> **KEY POINT**   The phenomenon of 'transference' occurs at a more superficial relational level than a meeting at 'relational depth' in person-centred counselling. The aim of the person-centred counsellor is to get through the client's 'transference process' in order to gain contact in his 'existential process'.

16 Brief companionship

BRIAN THORNE

Person-centred counsellors have tended to recoil in horror from the notion of brief counselling. Such a concept with its built-in assumption of a fixed number of sessions can seem to strike at the very heart of the client's right to self determination. The suspicion is that it puts all the power in the hands of the counsellor or allows an impersonal system to decree when counselling shall end irrespective of the actual wishes or needs of the client. What is more it makes apparent nonsense of the belief in a therapeutic process which develops at its own pace and in accordance with the client's readiness to take the risks which real growth must inevitably involve.

I must confess that these objections featured largely in my own thinking for many years and I believe that, by and large, they remain valid. If, for example, an institution or an agency for which I worked insisted that I could only offer short-term counselling for a stipulated number of sessions to all my clients irrespective of need I believe I would have no option but to resign.

A few years ago, however, in the face of an ever-escalating waiting list in the university counselling service of which I was then director, I found myself pursuing a very heretical line of thought. Whether through inspiration or desperation I do not know, but I dared to think the unthinkable. Could it be, I wondered, that there were some prospective clients for whom short-term counselling was not only a possible option but the most desirable and potentially the most effective? I was strengthened in this wayward reflection by the knowledge that the *average* number of sessions for clients using the Counselling Service was only five and that some seemed to go on their way rejoicing after a mere two or three meetings. An amusing afterthought was that in the literature, and especially in the psychodynamic tradition, short-term counselling usually means a mere 20 to 30 sessions!

After much internal agonising and against the better judgement of several colleagues, I moved from thinking the unthinkable to doing it. At the beginning of the summer term it was explained to would-be clients during their 'exploratory interview' (30 minutes of preliminary discussion which every person coming to the Service was offered) that there was a new option on the therapeutic menu. I called it *focused counselling* and those opting for it were offered three sessions only with the possibility of subsequent participation in a small group (consisting of focused counselling 'graduates') if they felt they still had further business to do. It was also explained that, although the basic mode of counselling offered in the three sessions would not differ fundamentally from the usual person-centred approach to which the Service is committed, the counsellor would be respectful of the client's desire to work rapidly and would offer a high level of empathic responsiveness from the outset with an emphasis on helping the client to clarify thoughts and feelings and to establish a sense of direction. It was further explained that because 'focused counselling' constituted a new initiative for a Service already heavily timetabled, sessions would be offered before the start of the normal working day at 8.15 a.m. It was likely, too, that those choosing focused counselling would not have to wait as long as those on the 'normal' waiting list. The response of those coming for exploratory sessions was fascinating. Most rejected the new option at once as unlikely to meet their needs. Some, tempted by the possibility of a reduced waiting period, considered it briefly only to back off at the prospect of the heightened concentration which appeared to be required and the thought of so early a start to the working day! There were, however, a small number of individuals (eight in all over a four-week period) who immediately seized the opportunity enthusiastically and declared that this was precisely the kind of counselling they were looking for. To make matters more bewildering, the concerns of this small minority ranged over a wide spectrum and some of the difficulties seemed to warrant far more than the contracted three sessions. I began the experiment with deep foreboding.

The first 'focused counselling' client arrived at 8.10 a.m. looking as if he had been up and about for some time. He began by saying that he had been struggling with a major life crisis for some weeks and needed to come to a resolution. In brief, he had to decide whether or not to continue his post-graduate degree, whether to change career, whether to commit himself to a single life or to settle down to marriage. With amazing rapidity he sketched out the psychological terrain, explored many of the accompanying feelings prompted by each potential solution and began to formulate a hierarchy of values. As the counsellor, I felt swept up into a process which was already well advanced. The client seemed to trust me from the first minute and I felt myself electrified into a level of attentiveness which was almost intoxicating. I have little doubt that I was empathically on top form and I felt utterly free to be myself in the service of so highly motivated a client. After 50 minutes, clarity was emerging and the client was beginning to smile with relief.

In many ways, this first session was typical of much that happened during my focused counselling relationships.

The clients themselves were characterised by a number of common features, many of which were exemplified by the man I have just described:

1. They were all highly motivated to work rapidly and intensively.
2. They had all been engaged in 'self-therapy' for some time and were therefore well advanced in their processes both of feeling and understanding.
3. They were prepared to trust me as the counsellor from the outset and with minimal 'testing of the waters'.
4. They had at least a modicum of self-regard however bruising their life's experience.
5. They were all skilled in the use of language.
6. None were isolated socially but all lacked an intimate relationship where they felt safe to be fully themselves.

Whatever they had in common, however, these eight clients presented an astonishing variety of concerns. Nor were their difficulties in any sense superficial or merely situational. Among them were delayed grief, the aftermath of rape, parental physical abuse, performance phobia in a performing arts student and the struggle to escape from a fundamentalist religious sect. In only one case did the client feel at the end of the three sessions that there was more essential work to be done and I agreed to continue working with her on an individual basis, no small group having emerged from the other clients who were all content to finish on schedule. In the event, this one client terminated after a further three sessions although both she and I agreed that there was more to be done at a future date when and if she felt the need to return.

Clearly it would be inappropriate to draw authoritative conclusions from so small a sample but certain lines of thought seemed legitimate at the time and have been reinforced by subsequent experience. In summary:

1. These clients were all self-exploring people who intuited immediately that brief counselling would meet their needs.
2. They required a particular kind of companionship to enable them to complete a process which was already well advanced.
3. Person-centred counselling offered them that companionship in a quintessential form.

It is my conviction that person-centred counselling at its best offers both intimacy and the possibility of mutuality. These clients, it seemed, adequately functioning as they were, lacked the intimacy where they could be fully trusting of the other. The therapeutic context enabled them to risk such intimacy from the outset. What is more their high level of motivation and their preparedness to commit themselves wholeheartedly to the task made it possible for me as the counsellor to experience an immediate level of mutuality where I could deploy the fullness of my own being without the fear either of making mistakes or of overwhelming the other. It was an experience which I have since repeated on many other occasions and almost always with equally beneficial results. Where a client generally opts for brief work of this kind and is not forced into such a contract, it would seem that he or she can be trusted to use the opportunity to the full. The intimacy and mutuality provided by the counsellor's companionship, together with his or her capacity to offer the core conditions in an intense and disciplined way, provides all that is required to enable the highly motivated client to make it to the next temporary destination on life's journey.

> **KEY POINT** A 'brief' approach to person-centred counselling can be appropriate for clients who consciously and deliberately *choose* that option and where the counsellor can manifest strong levels of the therapeutic conditions immediately and consistently.

17 Becoming aware of the 'unspoken relationship' between counsellor and client

One of the great paradoxes of counselling is the fact that it is characterised as such an open relationship and yet most of the ways in which the two people experience each other remain unspoken (Mearns, 1991a). Books which explore the client's experience of counselling show that many of the thoughts and feelings which the client had about the work, particularly about the relationship with the counsellor, remained unspoken throughout the process (Dinnage, 1987; Mearns and Dryden, 1989).

The person-centred approach emphasises the importance of the therapeutic relationship between counsellor and client and the active use of that relationship to highlight and explore aspects of the client's social and emotional functioning that are manifested in the therapeutic relationship. This makes it crucial for the person-centred counsellor to be able to find ways of using as much of that relationship as possible. Those parts of the therapeutic relationship that are most difficult to access may be particularly productive of therapeutic material.

A second important reason for attending to the therapeutic relationship is to maintain the health of that relationship. Any relationship which is left unattended is in danger of atrophy: that danger is greater where the client has already developed self-defeating patterns to his relating.

Despite this rationale for attending to the therapeutic relationship, it is still a relatively rare occurrence for counsellor and client to speak openly about the ways in which they experience each other in the work. In analysing 80 audiotaped sessions of first, second and third year trainee counsellors over a seven-year period 1 have recorded only two short interactions where the counsellor invited comment from the client on how he experienced the counsellor. Interestingly, in these tapes, there were 16 parallel invitations from the clients. Admittedly, a trainee counsellor might not have the confidence to be able to tap the thus far 'unspoken relationship' between herself and the client, but there is little evidence through supervision that experienced person-centred counsellors are any more proficient or willing to explore that territory. Aspects of the unspoken relationship between client and counsellor do surface but often by accident, for example, the client who revealed his assumption about the counsellor through his surprise at her negligence in arriving late for a session:

Client: Funnily enough, I was quite pleased that you were late for the session ... I always presumed that you were too *scared* of me to do anything wrong like being late.

Box 17.1 illustrates some examples of quite different perceptions that counsellors and clients held about the same events. These inconsistencies were part of the relationships between the two people and, if they had been exposed, they might not only have helped the relationships to strengthen through greater understanding but some would have raised therapeutic material for the client while others might have provided useful learning for the counsellor. An example of the raising of therapeutic material is the client who presumes that the counsellor would be experiencing her as 'just not trying'.

Where did this assumption come from and why is it established when the counsellor is, in fact, experiencing the opposite? This almost certainly leads directly to introjected material that would be therapeutically useful if it could be tapped. On the other hand, the counsellor who perceived the client's behaviour as 'a real catharsis' might learn considerably from the fact that the client had been aware that his emotional expression was not as real as it appeared.

The dynamics within the unspoken relationship merit examination. In *any* close relationship, therapeutic or otherwise, there is a gradual laying down of unvoiced reactions and assumptions: 'He must have done this because ...'; 'I suppose she must know what we're doing – she looks so confident'; 'I didn't understand what she said – I must be stupid'. These assumptions are our attempts to make sense of our world. It is vital that we make these assumptions, even if they are wrong, because we need to feel that our social world is broadly *consistent* and *predictable*. That gives us the experience, or at least the illusion, of safety. The battery of assumptions that we build up about the other in a relationship comprises the largely *unspoken shield* that interprets the other's behaviour and protects us from the reality of that behaviour which may be inconsistent with our assumptions (see Figure 17.1).

Box 17.1

Some examples of misperceptions between clients and counsellors

Counsellors tend to be both confident about the clarity of their own behaviour in relation to the client and also of the accuracy of their perceptions of the client. However, explorations of the *unspoken relationship* between the two can throw up many examples of misperception. The examples which follow are simultaneous thoughts of the client and the counsellor. These thoughts were not voiced until later in counselling. We might say that these are thoughts from the 'unspoken relationship' between counsellor and client.

Client: She [*the counsellor*] thinks I'm just not trying.
Counsellor: I think she's a real fighter.

Counsellor: He [*the client*] must be getting something out of this – he keeps coming!
Client: Maybe if I keep coming I'll eventually get something out of this!

Client: She knows what I should do, but she isn't telling me!
Counsellor: God knows what she should do!

Counsellor: He [*the client*] is at ease with me now.
Client: I still think she's a witch!

Counsellor: That was a real catharsis!
Client: I wasn't really being 'real' there – it was all a bit of an 'act'.

Even early in a relationship there is a vast amount of communication occurring between the two people at many different levels. Human beings are wondrous in the skills they possess including the skills to deceive each other and themselves in order to preserve the illusion of predictability and safety in their social worlds. In relationship with each other they form *norms*: accepted ways of behaving and attitudes. These norms define and therefore stabilise the relationship. The norms hold the relationship together, but the 'cement' they provide can become *restrictive* to future development and change.

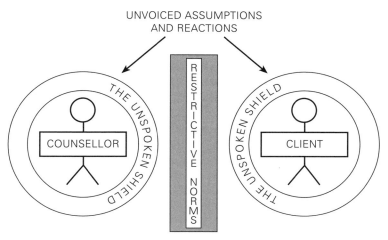

Figure 17.1

The build-up of *restrictive norms* in the therapeutic relationship will be distinctive to that relationship; however, some of these norms are sufficiently common that we can list them below as a way of stimulating the counsellor's reflection:

- The client stops bringing his or her *most* fearful issues.
- The client 'works the edge off' issues before voicing them.
- The counsellor continues to be supportive, but becomes less challenging.
- The counsellor stops working with relationship difficulties in relation to the client.
- There is a reduction of 'here and now' material introduced by both client and counsellor.
- They become stuck in a safe cognitive domain.
- They become stuck in a safe affective domain (stuck in old, well-worked feelings rather than 'edge of awareness' feelings).
- The counselling sessions develop an internal *pattern* which tends to be replayed session after session.

Figure 17.1 gives a representational view of the protections and barriers created by the restrictive norms and unspoken shields of both persons. This is a stable, defensive state into which relationships will tend to drift unless or until the pattern is challenged by the individuals concerned. Challenging this pattern is substantially the responsibility of the counsellor because she is the professional in the room. Yet, 'tapping the unspoken relationship' is a delicate matter, as described in the next section.

> **KEY POINT** Even in person-centred counselling a large part of the relationship between counsellor and client is unspoken. Laying down unspoken assumptions about each other and developing implicit norms in the relationship are normal ways of creating predictability and safety in the relationship. However, that unspoken relationship contains material which is of great potential therapeutic importance.

18 Tapping the 'unspoken relationship' between counsellor and client

When the counsellor seeks to explore the unspoken relationship between herself and her client she is breaking the conventions of communication. As described in Section 17, many of the ways in which two people experience each other in a relationship remain unspoken in order to preserve the consistency and stability of the relationship. When the counsellor invites the client to open the door to those unspoken parts the client may feel some discomfort and could even deny access. Of course, it is not only the client who may feel that discomfort: perhaps one of the reasons why even person-centred counsellors only rarely explore the unspoken relationship relates to the discomfort which they feel about entering the unknown in their relationships.

The supervisor can have a positive influence on the counsellor in terms of exploring the unspoken relationship. Unfortunately, the way this often arises is in situations where the unspoken relationship problems have grown to such an extent that the counsellor is worried about his or her work with that client. Where a person-centred counsellor presents the supervisor with such concerns the following two questions may prove to be fruitful: 'How is the *client* experiencing the work you are doing?' and 'Might you be more *congruent* in relation to this client?' (Mearns, 1991b). The first question alerts the counsellor to the fact that she may be unsure about how the client is experiencing the work and perhaps also that she has been avoiding addressing the issue with the client. The second question is an intentionally leading one because the person-centred counsellor who gets into relationship difficulties with a client is almost always incongruent whether as a cause or an effect of the difficulty. When there is difficulty in a relationship, the immediate self-protective tendency is to pull oneself slightly out of the relationship. Usually it takes an act of intention to become more congruent in the relationship (Mearns, 1992a).

When the counsellor seeks to explore the unspoken relationship with a client she must be particularly respectful in her approach. Firmly demanding that the client discloses his unspoken assumptions and expectations about the counsellor is likely to create further unspoken relationship problems rather than bring to the surface any which already exist. A better procedure is for the counsellor to initiate the process by disclosing some of her own uncertainties or assumptions and seeking to check these with the client. This is a gentle way of inviting the client into the unspoken areas offered in a sufficiently respectful fashion that the client can still decline, often by denying that there is an issue. Sometimes the counsellor will find that the client does not respond to the first invitation but raises the issue himself at a later opportunity: 'I was thinking about what you said last time and I suppose there really is a difficulty there ...'.

There are both structured and unstructured ways of tapping the unspoken relationship. 'Review' sessions provide excellent structured opportunities for exploring the unspoken relationship. Such reviews might usefully explore the areas represented by the six boxes in Figure 18.1, noting particularly those items which unearth differing perceptions or assumptions between the client and the counsellor.

The template offered in Figure 18.1 is distinctly person-centred in character, with the emphasis on the three elements of the work: client, counsellor and the relationship between the two. Although the prime focus of the work is the client, attention needs to be given to all three in reviewing person-centred process.

Kagan's Interpersonal Process Recall method (Kagan, 1984) has been much adapted to be helpful in research and training as well as in counselling itself. The central idea of the method can also be used as a way to uncover aspects of the unspoken relationship. A tape-recording of a whole session or part of a session is replayed and made the basis of

	Impact of the work on the client	Impact of the work on the counsellor	The nature of the client–counsellor relationship
Client perception			
Counsellor perception			

Figure 18.1 A template for counselling review sessions

a future session with counsellor and client sharing their reflections on elements of the taped session as these unfold. Immediately, this process takes both participants to the level of reflecting on the perspectives they held in the taped session. Each is able to explain to the other the feelings which were being experienced by them in the moment and how these compare or contrast with their actual expressions of feeling. This is a powerful method which can create an enormous amount of therapeutic material because it gets so directly at the assumptions which each of the people are holding about the other and about the work. The client and counsellor are engaging in 'meta-communication', a process well explored in research and practice within the 'process-experiential' part of the person-centred 'family' of therapies. An excellent introduction to this discipline is offered by David Rennie (1998).

Another structured way of exploring aspects of the unspoken relationship is to adapt Laing's Interpersonal Perception Method (IPM) (Laing, Phillipson and Lee, 1966). The basic principle in this method is that each of the two persons in the relationship should respond to the same questions, giving his or her own answers and also endeavouring to predict how the other will answer. As in Kagan's method, this immediately takes the participants to other levels of perspective.

In Table 18.1, both the counsellor and the client, John, responded with a tick or a cross to indicate agreement (or predicted agreement) as opposed to disagreement (or predicted disagreement) with each statement. Even these few statements create an interesting pattern for John and his counsellor to analyse. For example, they found a full understanding about the fact that John was more depressed than last year (2), but also that he was more hopeful about his life (1). The fact that both counsellor and client not only shared the same opinions on these items

Table 18.1

		1 Client's answer	2 Counsellor's answer	3 Counsellor's prediction of client's answer	4 Client's prediction of counsellor's answer
1	John is more hopeful about his life	✓	✓	✓	✓
2	John is more depressed than last year	✓	✓	✓	✓
3	John is more anxious than last year	✗	✗	✗	✗
4	John is fearful about the future	✓	✗	✗	✗
5	John likes himself more than last year	✗	✓	✓	✓
6	John is getting stronger	✓	✓	✗	✓
7	John copes better at work	✓	✓	✓	✓
8	John copes better socially	✗	✓	✓	✓

but correctly understood the other's view represented a sophisticated level of understanding. The background to this point was that when John first came into counselling he was so split off from his feelings that he exhibited broadly psychotic symptoms. Becoming more depressed represented a greater contact with reality than before. Hence, while he was more 'depressed', he was also more 'hopeful'. This is the kind of observation that emphasises the importance of taking a phenomenological perspective on clinical outcomes – of actually seeking to understand outcomes in terms of the client's experiences. On conventional measures of outcome, like the Beck Depression Inventory, John would be seen as regressing, but that is the opposite of John's experience. This kind of finding reinforces an emphasis of the researcher, Stephen Goss, that counselling evaluations generally require a 'pluralist' methodology where qualitative and quantitative measures are informed by each other and the overall products can be meaningful to a variety of stakeholders (Goss and Mearns, 1997a and b).

Item 3 shows that both counsellor and client had a full understanding of the fact that John's anxiety had reduced but item 4 is interesting in that the counsellor did not believe that John was fearful about the future (column 2) and also did not realise (column 3) that John would report that fear (column 1). This item becomes even more revealing when we see from the entry in the fourth column that the client accurately predicted the counsellor's misunderstanding on this issue. In other words, the client is fearful about the future and also knows that this is an aspect of himself which is not yet understood in the counselling.

In item 5 the counsellor's judgement is interesting. The counsellor believes that there has been a positive movement in terms of John's self-acceptance (column 2) but he correctly predicts (column 3) that this will not be reported by John himself. John, on the other hand, expected the counsellor to see him the way he saw himself (column 4). In item 6, on the other hand, the counsellor's entry in the third column suggests that he thought John would not appreciate the fact that he was getting 'stronger' when, in fact, the client did appreciate the point (column 1) and expected it to be perceived by the counsellor (column 4).

There is full understanding of the fact that John is managing better at work (7) but on the social front (8) the client discloses that he does not feel an improvement (column 1) and, interestingly, he correctly predicts (column 4) that the counsellor would not be aware of that perception.

Even from this sample of eight IPM items we can see its potential for bringing more into the open the ways in which both the counsellor and the client are experiencing each other. The IPM can be as long as both people wish and it may also include items pertaining to the counsellor. Deriving the statements is best achieved through discussion so that the exploration is truly shared rather than imposed by the counsellor. The IPM can be combined with a review session and can be presented as a fun way of exploring how well each person can predict the views of the other. Indeed, students sometimes take the principle of the IPM home to explore with their partner.

Review sessions as well as the IPR and IPM methods are structured approaches to exploring elements within the unspoken relationship. However, person-centred counselling can also make use of unstructured means of eliciting and comparing the ways in which client and counsellor are experiencing the relationship. Sometimes this is initiated by the client questioning the counsellor, but it also arises through the *congruent* response of the counsellor to the client, for example, it may be initiated through the counsellor giving voice to an uncertainty or discomfort:

Counsellor: I've been wondering . . . in the last few weeks it has felt like you are pulling away a little . . . that you aren't so 'engaged' in our work than you were before? . . . Is there anything in that?

Client: I'm 'engaged' all right – it's nothing to do with *me!*

The reader will guess, even from this very short extract of dialogue, that there was indeed some difficulty in the unspoken relationship between the counsellor and client. In this instance, most of the material was housed in the client. Briefly, what emerged after one or two fairly lengthy silences was that the client had been heavily influenced by a recent discussion with a friend who had cast doubt upon counselling in general and this counsellor in particular. This raised two issues that were to prove of crucial therapeutic importance for the client. First, the client was able to reflect upon the fact that when doubt had begun to enter his mind, he moved in an instant from being highly positive about the counsellor to the polar opposite. The therapeutic dividend in this was the later realisation that this had been his pattern in relationships throughout his life: people were 'saints' until one small thing went wrong, whereupon they became 'sinners'. The second part of the therapeutic dividend was that this incident led the client to realise that he had been feeling powerfully unstable about the great amount of change which had already taken place in him through the counselling process. He was at that difficult stage in the process when the client realises that he is changing so much as a person that some aspects of his life are probably going to have to follow. At that very shaky time there had been a possibility that the client would reject the whole process in order to protect the self (see Section 22). In this example the counsellor's congruent confrontation thus proved to be crucial to the therapeutic process in its unveiling of vital aspects of the unspoken relationship and in its turn revealing further therapeutic material.

Perhaps one of the reasons why even person-centred counsellors do not tap the unspoken relationship as much as they might is that when we explore the unknown in a relationship, we do not know what we are going to uncover. While the above example led to discoveries on the part of the client, it is sometimes the counsellor who does the learning! That seems an appropriate point at which to end this brief introduction to the twilight zone of the unspoken relationship.

> **KEY POINT**   Tapping the unspoken relationship between counsellor and client is a matter for gentle invitation. If the client wishes to embark on the exploration there are both structured and unstructured means.

IV

The Therapeutic Process

19 Getting the 'power dynamic' right

The issue of 'power' is fundamental to person-centred counselling. Indeed, the essential principle of the person-centred approach is that the counsellor does not take responsibility for the client but encourages the client to find and exercise his own power.

Although power is so central to person-centred counselling, it is also an issue that is widely misunderstood. Often power is seen solely in terms of specific counsellor behaviours so the trainee person-centred counsellor becomes scared to make suggestions, offer interpretations, confront, theorise or offer advice, seeing these as the manifestations of taking power in the relationship. Such a trainee counsellor might be amazed to see an experienced person-centred practitioner in action with a long-standing client. The trainee would be surprised to see how assertive and active the counsellor could be, even at times offering suggestions, interpretations, theoretical observations and certainly being confronting. The trainee would also be surprised to see how those behaviours did not appear to usurp the client's power – the client could consider these various offerings quite openly, taking what was relevant and discarding the rest. *Both* the client and the counsellor could be powerful and active within the relationship while the client remained not just the centre of attention but also the centre of his own evaluation. In this case the counsellor and client have achieved the appropriate *'power dynamic'* for person-centred work: the nature of power within the therapeutic relationship is such that the client has come to see himself as the most important judge and arbiter in his life, with the counsellor in the position of consultant creating a context where the client can review his options.

The aim of the person-centred counsellor is to establish this kind of power dynamic. Achieving this is not merely a question of the counsellor avoiding various 'power behaviours' (see Section 20): power is a relationship issue and the dynamic is only achieved if the counsellor is both able to resist imposing her own power and is able to help the client to explore any tendencies he may have to give his power away.

One way in which clients may give their power away is through *transference*. As was described in Section 15, the person-centred counsellor will not encourage the development of transference and, indeed, she will work towards bringing transference issues into the open. Thus, the client can learn about any such tendencies he has to give his power away within the therapeutic relationship. This exercises the client's taking of responsibility and further contributes to the establishment of the right power dynamic.

That power dynamic is also furthered by the person-centred counsellor's resistance to taking responsibility *for* the client, though the counsellor will be resolute in her willingness to be responsible *to* the client. This is a simple yet crucial distinction and one which the person-centred counsellor can use to guide most of her actions in relationship with the client. The counsellor will avoid taking responsibility *for* the client in even small ways like naming the client's feelings; determining the frequency of sessions; and speculating on the overall length and steps of the counselling process. On the other hand, the person-centred counsellor will be most diligent in being responsible *to* the client. In this regard the counsellor will take great care to be on time for sessions; not to foreshorten the length of sessions; to be consistently attentive to the client; to be respectful of the client; and to seek to establish the therapeutic conditions within the relationship no matter how difficult that might be. It is these dimensions of responsibility which ensure that the counsellor is offering a reliable service to the client.

It is sometimes argued, even by person-centred counsellors, that it is acceptable to allow some degree of client *dependency* during the early stages of the process but then to wean the client away from that dependency when he is in less need. The disadvantage in this procedure is that by encouraging a dependency process at all the counsellor may be severely elongating the work because, in practice, it is not easy to transform a dependent relationship into one in which the client is self-sufficient. The alternative to accepting this dependency relationship does not mean being harsh or rejecting and dismissive of the client's needs. Being consistently responsible *to* the client without accepting responsibility *for* him is a gentle and caring position that reflects a great valuing of the client. Person-centred counsellors can learn a considerable amount about this climate of being responsible *to* the client rather than *for* him through the literature on the ways of working of the child-centred play therapist who is concerned to establish exactly that relationship even with young children. If the child can thus be encouraged to become his own locus of evaluation without needing the therapist to take responsibility for him even in the beginning, then so too can the adult client (Axline, 1964; Ginsberg, 1984; West, 1992).

The counsellor may 'tap the unspoken relationship' (see Section 18) in order to check on the power dynamic. Issues to do with dependency, responsibility and transference often lie quite deep in the therapeutic relationship, having their bases as they do in the needs and fears of the client and sometimes the counsellor. The extract which follows, and closes this section, illustrates how the counsellor used her congruent expression of her own fear to tap the unspoken relationship between herself and the client. Quite quickly it becomes apparent that the relationship had been slipping into one in which the client was giving much of his own responsibility for himself to the counsellor. That was particularly dangerous in this case because the client had developed a pattern of, in his own words, 'playing with the possibility of suicide'. The following is only a small extract taken from quite a long exploration. This session had been preceded a few nights earlier by a phone call from the client after he had once again toyed with the mechanics of his suicide.

Counsellor: I'm pleased that you phoned the other night ... but I felt uneasy when you were off the phone. I would like us to talk about how we both see our work together. My worry is that you may see me as more of a support than I can really be.

Client: I'm scared now – scared that you are pulling away.

Counsellor: Maybe you are right, in the sense that I think I'm pulling away from what you see as my role in our work. I mean ... when we got off the phone I found myself trembling – I was pretty scared.

Client: You were scared!

Counsellor: Yes – I was frightened that you were maybe putting too much weight onto me – that you were maybe even risking your life in the belief that I could *save* you.

Client: It makes me feel scared to hear that you were scared.

Counsellor: That's perhaps the point that we're getting at, John – maybe we have been creating the illusion that I can make things *safe* for you. I really can't make things safe for you. That's *your* power, *your* choice – your life is *your* choice. I can, and I will, stay close to you, but I can't hold you up – I can't save your life.

Client: Maybe I've known that all along – but maybe I've been trying to get you to hold me up ... I feel alone and scared now.

Counsellor: That sounds pretty real.

Client: Yes ... *cold* reality.

> **KEY POINT** Always keep in mind that you are aiming to establish the kind of 'power dynamic' with the client that helps him to exercise and develop his own power rather than lean on yours.

20 Let the client's locus of evaluation be the guide to your working

June: Do you do exorcism?

It was an unusual beginning to a first session with a new client. But what followed was just as bizarre and made sense of the beginning.

June: I have an 'Abused Child' inside me, and it's not mine.
Counsellor: Whose is it?
June: I think it belongs to my previous therapist. 'Abused Inner Children' were her 'thing' and I think she gave one to me.

Unfortunately, we cannot continue this description in dialogue since first sessions are never taped and I am operating from memory and notes. Briefly, June described how she had come to me partly because I worked in a different city and partly because I was a man. In work with a previous therapist she had found herself believing that she had been sexually abused as an infant. She reported that her therapist had referred to this as 'pre-verbal sexual abuse' and that it was a way to understand her constant anxiety, her inability to sustain relationships and her lack of sexual response. She reported that her therapist had repeatedly sought to address her 'Abused Inner Child' (the therapist's terminology). June had found herself responding to these requests first by crying a lot and then by 'making up' (her words) vague sensations and images, pieced together from things she had read, but also including some emotional reactions which she could not relate to anything. She began to wonder what was reality and what was not. Perhaps she really had been sexually abused as an infant? From her report of that period in therapy, it sounded as though she had come close to psychosis. Also, in one session she had imagined a large man coming towards her then the experience of physical pain – then darkness. But she had no idea whether it was a real memory or imagined. By this time she had lost sight of why she had come into therapy, but she had left her partner and now lived alone, totally devoting herself to 'uncovering her Abused Inner Child'. She reported that her therapist had introduced notions such as 'ritualised sexual abuse' and 'multiple personality'. She also noted that her therapist had said that 'most of my clients have been sexually abused as children'.

June read a newspaper article referring to 'false memory syndrome' and raised the question of this with her therapist, also confessing that she had 'made some things up'. She wondered if perhaps she had not really been abused as a child? She reported her therapist's response as 'It would be nice to believe that, wouldn't it?'

Working with June tested every element of my person-centred approach. I was very strict in my working, relying only on partial or accurate empathy, being entirely congruent in response to her, never introducing any things of my own, and never presuming that I understood her. At times it was better to work with her using pre-therapy reflections (see Sections 29 and 30) as she lost 'contact' with her affect and with me for brief periods. Throughout my work with her I was aware that the power dynamic (see Section 19) in the relationship was absolutely crucial. Her *locus of evaluation* (Raskin, 1952) was so externalised that, in the beginning, she had difficulty in even making judgements about the nature of her own feelings and sensations. She behaved like a person who had lost confidence, or who never had confidence in her self and yet, on occasions, she exhibited a surprisingly strong sense of self underlying the 'lost' way of being which was on the surface. Perhaps that underlying strong sense of self had helped her to leave her previous therapy and to make some of the decisions which came later.

The person-centred approach worked well with June: in fact, I was certain that the person-centred approach was the *only* way of working with such a client since her locus of evaluation was so removed from herself. Any elements of directivity which were out of line with her experiencing would be internalised as reality at the expense of her own valuing process.

Our work together was slow and painstaking. She systematically considered every feeling, belief or assumption that she had made about herself and endeavoured to re-examine these. Sometimes she was able to decide which of them were hers and which were not, but much of the time they had to remain in the 'undecided' category. In terms of person-centred Self Theory, what she was doing was filtering through all the elements in her self-structure, endeavouring to decide which of these tallied with her experience and which had been introjected from a variety of sources including her mother, her teachers and her previous therapist. In terms of the Self Theory, it would have been logical also to look at the re-integration of denied experiences, but she never introduced any such material and I was certainly not going to explore the denied area since she was highly vulnerable to the slightest suggestion.

Interestingly, she made some pretty big decisions which came entirely from herself and about which she felt very good. She started work again and also she invited her former partner to dinner. It was never possible to start that relationship again but making the connection once more was extremely comforting for her.

I learned a considerable amount about counselling through my work with June. The main thing I learned was how important it is to be aware of the power dynamic in relation to a client and to be very careful about the individual difference between clients. In Section 19, reference was made to the fact that the person-centred counsellor can become freer in his or her expression when the power dynamic is such that the client has substantially internalised his locus of evaluation. In working with June, that point was never reached. Although, at the end of her work, she was a little more at the centre of her locus of evaluation, for much of our time together she was potentially very vulnerable to being deflected from her own valuing process by the slightest presumption the counsellor might make about her experiencing. This work with June illustrates one of the most important points about person-centred work: *that it is largely governed by the nature of the client's locus of evaluation*. If that locus is markedly externalised the counsellor needs to be aware that the client will be vulnerable to any externally provided ways of defining himself. Where the counsellor would feel more free with a client who had substantially internalised his locus of evaluation and was achieving a degree of mutuality in the relationship, she would be more cautious of the possibility of directivity with the client whose locus of evaluation was profoundly externalised. While this may sound like a straightforward equation by which we decide how to work with our client, it still begs the question of how we assess the client's locus of evaluation and how quickly we can do that. In fact, the client with a profoundly externalised locus of evaluation will show that very quickly. Within minutes the counsellor will feel the client looking to her for the needed definition of his self. The more difficult example is the client whose different 'configurations' of self (Section 4; Mearns, 1999; Mearns and Thorne, 2000) have varying loci for their self-evaluations. In Chapter 7 of *Person-Centred Therapy Today* (Mearns and Thorne, 2000), the client 'Clair' is introduced. We find that she describes two 'configurations' which she names as 'my strong self' and 'my little girl'. In his case notes the author comments on the mistakes he makes with respect to locus of evaluation:

> I can't believe how I missed Clair's 'little girl' for so long. Her 'strong self' just got together with my 'strong self' and there was no space for her 'little girl'. Also, while her 'strong self' had a fairly inter-nalised locus of evaluation that was certainly not the case for her 'little girl' – her 'little girl' even found it difficult to exist without reference to her 'strong self'. I jumped straight in with a fairly strong relationship with part of Clair – but I really needed to be more cautious until I had met all of her.

So, the person-centred counsellor might fairly easily recognise a profoundly externalised locus of evaluation, but other cases are not so straightforward. Hence a better counsellor than Mearns with Clair would be cautious with a strongly presenting client until she had met all of him.

In the clearer situation, where the profoundly externalised locus of evaluation is easily seen, as in the case of June, the person-centred coun-sellor would take particular care not to introduce her own ideas, intuitions, spirituality, values or realities or to interpret the client's expe-rience in any way whatsoever.

By way of a footnote to this section I want to emphasise that the expe-rience of June and her uncertainty about the reality of her own childhood abuse should not be taken to suggest that sexual abuse in infancy or ritu-alised sexual abuse do not exist or are exaggerated. These phenomena do exist and are generally much more widespread than people care to believe.

KEY POINT   Where the client has an externalised locus of evaluation the counsellor must take extreme care not to compound that vulnerability by introducing material of her own.

21 Assisting the client's focusing

Section 19 emphasised the value of achieving the right 'power dynamic' for person-centred working. That is a pivotal issue in the work: if the right power dynamic is achieved then the client will retain responsibility for himself and the counsellor can be as assertive as she likes without fear of the client being over-awed. In this regard Section 20 is cautionary because it points to the opposite situation, where the client's locus of evaluation is so externalised that the counsellor must be aware of how easy it would be for her own power to over-awe and mislead the client. In both these situations the counsellor needs to be able to help the client to *focus on his own* process so that he can come to understand it, begin to own it and delve deeper into it. An introduction to focusing within person-centred counselling is given in Mearns and Thorne (1999: 52–58). A sizeable literature on focusing exists both in its application within person-centred counselling (Gendlin, 1984) and as a study in its own right (Gendlin, 1981; 1996).

When integrated within person-centred counselling, 'focusing' is essentially about helping the client *to empathise with himself*. It is an unobtrusive invitation to the client to move toward the edge of his awareness in exploring an issue. Important therapeutic movements can result as the client reaches the edge of his awareness: for example, the client may discover the true *intensity* of feeling which is related to that issue or that the feeling which had been on the surface was actually masking quite a *different* feeling underneath. Fresh awareness such as this can totally change the direction of exploration and may even help the client to further the therapeutic process by discovering earlier denied experiences or introjected aspects of self structure. Brief moments of focusing can have major consequences in the change of direction which they facilitate.

Assisting the client's focusing in person-centred counselling is not achieved by the counsellor learning focusing 'techniques'. Essential to the process is the depth of the counsellor's engagement with the client at the edge of the client's awareness (see Section 2). If the client does not experience the counsellor's engagement in this way then any focusing responses the counsellor makes will sound hollow and uninviting. Clients need to feel more than the 'technical' expertise of the counsellor if they are going to open themselves to potentially disturbing discoveries. When the counsellor *is* close to the experiencing of the client she will explore the edge of that awareness by means of a variety of verbal and non-verbal responses, all of which reflect the client back to himself so that he can see the *resonance* or otherwise between what he is expressing and his underlying feeling. In this way the client is assisted in testing and improving the *congruence* between his underlying feelings and his expression of feelings. In the course of achieving that congruence the client and counsellor are also able to observe the operation of the client's self-protective mechanisms which may have disguised the intensity of the underlying feeling or even transposed the true feeling into some other, 'safer' feeling.

It is difficult to give brief examples of focusing in counselling because the sense of the counsellor's response is only really understood by transcribing much of what has gone before. However, the reader might be able to use personal experience to imagine the kind of contexts in which the following examples of focusing could have arisen. Each of these six examples illustrates a different form of response of the counsellor. Once again we emphasise that the skill of helping clients to focus will not be obtained simply by learning these different responses but by developing the openness and ability to engage the client at relational depth.

1. *Word-for-word reflection*
   Client: ... so ... I just feel a bit depressed about it all ... that's all.
   Counsellor: ... so ... you just feel a bit depressed about it all ... that's all.
   Client: [*pause*] Shit ... That's not right at all ... I'm totally *devastated* about it.

One of the most simple and yet powerfully effective focusing responses is to present the client with an exact recording of what he has just said. Immediately on comparing that reflection with his underlying feeling he realised that he was completely understating the intensity. It goes without saying that this word for word reflection may lose its potency if overused (and the counsellor may be mistaken for a parrot!)

2. Reflection of the client's feeling or sensation using a 'handle word' (see Mearns and Thorne, 1999: 53)

> *Client:* ... I feel ... I don't know what I feel ... I feel [*stiffens body and face – straightens arms at side of body – eyes stare straight ahead*]
> *Counsellor:* ... You feel ... [*pause*] ... 'frozen'? You feel totally 'frozen' by it all?
> *Client:* Yes, 'frozen' – like I'm scared to behave in any way at all ... like *anything* I do might be wrong, so the only way to be is to be 'frozen' – to be 'stuck'.

In this example the client's sensation was not yet sufficiently familiar to him to be translated into language. The counsellor helped that process by offering a 'handle word' – a word which seemed, to the counsellor, to be descriptive of what the client was expressing physically. Such handle words are offered tentatively, with an implied question, so that the client resonates the handle word against his own experiencing and perhaps even improves upon the word. In this case 'frozen' was close to the client's experience and later was improved to 'stuck'. Now that the client had language for his experiencing, he was able to explore it further.

3. *Adding an emphasis with a questioning tone*
> *Client:* ... I suppose I am a bit upset about it.
> *Counsellor:* ... You are 'a bit upset' [*added emphasis*] about it?
> *Client:* [*pause*] Ha! It sounds funny when you say it back to me – 'a bit upset' – that sounds like a tea party compared to how I feel.

Sometimes it is simply so obvious that the client is understating the intensity of the feeling that the counsellor who is close to the client's experiencing can be more emphatic with the reflection in the knowledge that the client will readily become aware of the gulf between his expression and the underlying feeling. This more directive focusing response would not be given where the client's locus of evaluation was markedly externalised. In that case there would be a danger of the client switching tracks onto the counsellor's way of experiencing and going even farther away from 'focusing' on his own sense of self.

4. *Slowing the pace of response to the client*
> *Client:* [*speaking very fast*] And so I just said to him [his partner] – if you don't want our relationship then just forget it! – just let's both of us be free.
> *Counsellor:* [*speaking much more slowly*] You – just – said – to him. If – you – don't – want – our – relationship – then – just forget – it. Just – let's – both – of – us – be – free?
> *Client:* [*pause*] I guess ... being 'free' isn't how it *really* feels.

One way in which the client may protect himself from experiencing the full force of his feeling is by running past the feeling so quickly that he does not have time to pause and focus. In this example, all the counsellor did was to slow the client's speech and give it back to him at a pace which could be resonated with his underlying feeling. This immediately enabled the client to become aware that he was much more involved in his relationship than his words implied.

5. *Using 'touch' to invite the client to focus*
   Client: It doesn't matter what I do. I think I should just go away and die. The best thing I could do for my wife and children is just to go away and die.
   Counsellor: [*leans forward and touches the client gently on the hand, but says nothing.*]
   Client: [*looks at the counsellor and bursts into deep sobbing.*]

Although it is a rare event in person-centred counselling, the approach does not run away from touch as a powerful form of expression in relationships. A focusing touch communicates that the counsellor is aware of the power of what the client is expressing even if the client himself is not yet fully experiencing that power. The counsellor's touch also communicates a human *warmth* which carries its own impact.

6. Even silence on its own may help the client to focus
   Client: [*speaking very fast*] There's no way I'm going back into hospital – I can hold it together – I can manage – I'll die if I go back there – it will be the end of me – I'll kill the bastards before I go back there!
   Counsellor: [*continues to look at the client, but remains silent.*]
   Client: [*pause*] Jesus ... listen to me ... I didn't know how bad it was for me.

In this example the counsellor's silence provided the space for the client to slow down and hear himself.

Listing these various kinds of focusing responses may help the person-centred counsellor to reflect upon his or her own style and repertoire. One useful learning technique is for counsellors to replay audio- or videotapes of their own work in order to see how they have expressed their closeness to the client's underlying feeling. Perhaps some of the forms shown above might also have represented useful responses to the clients. Counsellors might also consider points on their tapes when they did not respond to the client in a focusing way but perhaps continued at the same pace as the client. In some of these instances it might have been helpful to change the pace for a moment in order to help the client to focus.

As has been emphasised earlier, these variants of a focusing response will only carry an impact if the counsellor is close to the client's experiencing and the client perceives that closeness. It is useless to endeavour to mimic these responses as a technique, because clients know the difference between a counsellor who is close to their experiencing and one whose level of commitment is limited to the disembodied use of 'techniques'.

KEY POINT Where the counsellor is close to the experiencing of the client various 'focusing' responses can help the client to attend to the edge of his awareness.

---

22 Be aware of and beware the dynamics of self-concept change

To understand the therapeutic process from a person-centred framework it is necessary to comprehend the dynamics which are involved in self-concept change. Inexperienced counsellors may be confused by the uneven nature of the therapeutic process where the client shows periods of movement but also times of apparent 'stuckness' and even regression. If the counsellor does not understand the nature of the self-concept change process within counselling there is a danger that she will not be able to offer a consistent relationship. An example of this is where the client enters a period of apparent 'stuckness' in the therapeutic relationship and the counsellor, not realising the significance of this in relation to self-concept change processes, forsakes the consistency of the person-centred framework and begins to try to 'move the client on' by whatever means. This happens all too often with counsellors whose person-centred training has only been superficial: when faced with apparent 'stuckness' they tend to introduce directive measures like exercises and techniques drawn from other counselling approaches. Improving our work as a person-centred counsellor involves understanding processes such as self-concept change so that we are less naive in our response to the client (see also Combs, 1989: Chapter 4).

Self-concept is our *attitude* towards our self. Like any attitude it has three components, commonly referred to as the *cognitive* component (our knowledge and beliefs about our self); an *affective* component (our feelings and evaluations about our self) and a *behavioural* component (our tendency to behave in ways which reflect our thoughts and feelings about our self).

The fact that an attitude contains such a wealth and variety of human experiencing adds to its strength, stability and resistance to change. That stability is further enhanced by the fact that the elements within an attitude tend to be internally *consistent* with each other; that is to say they will mostly reflect the same kind of evaluation or direction. This internal consistency creates a phenomenon which can be likened to the 'bundle of sticks' analogy. If we were to isolate any one specific opinion, belief or feeling then it might be challenged and changed relatively easily. However, the fact that the elements within an attitude are bound together with an internal consistency makes it difficult to change one element in isolation – essentially the whole attitude has to be changed or not at all.

Self-concept is an attitude just like any other: each of the specific opinions, beliefs, feelings and evaluations about our self might well be changeable if only we could get it in isolation, but we cannot. These elements are all bound up together and they support each other against the threat of change. Our client may not *like* his self-concept, but still that self-concept will seek to preserve itself by maintaining its internal consistency because inconsistency is a greater existential threat to the human being than simple negativity: we can cope with feeling bad about ourself more easily than we can cope with existential confusion. Naive attempts to change the client's attitude will have been offered by numerous helpful people in the past: they will have pointed out to him his good points and ways in which he is too hard upon himself. However, it is unlikely that these attempts at changing specific elements of his attitude will have been successful because the rest of his attitude will have repelled this invasion by contradictory feedback, finding ways to dismiss or devalue it. Thus, the consistency of the attitude towards self is preserved in the same way that consistency and homeostasis is maintained within the rest of the organism.

Person-centred counselling is important for self-concept change because it exacerbates *dissonance* within the attitude towards self. Dissonance is increased through three pathways. First, in the course of counselling, the client becomes aware of individual successes and achievements which have earlier been *denied*. The client's initial response is often to feel fearful of that awareness and even attempt to continue the denial process, yet, in the context of a person-centred counselling relationship, this awareness of previously denied elements which are inconsistent to a negative self-concept may become likened to the grains of sand which create the pearl in the oyster. They are initially small, dissonant but undeniable elements which run counter to the negative fear of the self-concept and, unless they are discounted by the reactionary forces of the self-concept, they will be influential towards change.

A second means by which the person-centred counselling process can create dissonance within the self-concept is through the re-evaluation of *introjected* material within the self structure. The client will have introjected numerous elements that reflect the overall negativity but which do not necessarily relate to the client's experience of himself. For example, the client may have introjected statements from parents that emphasised his lack of intellectual ability. In the course of person-centred counselling the client may become aware of the source of this aspect of the self-concept as belonging to introjected material rather than actual experience. Once again a dissonant grain of sand has been introduced into the negative self-concept and maintained by the continuation of counselling.

The third main pathway through which dissonance is increased in person-centred counselling is what Germain Lietaer describes as the 'counter-conditioning' effect of the counsellor's unconditional positive regard (Lietaer, 1984). While the client may portray an overall negativity in his or her self-concept, the counsellor does not collude with that judgement but continues to respond to the client with unconditional positive regard. Initially the client may be uncomfortable with that unconditional positive regard because, in his terms, he is not deserving of that regard. There may even be aspects of his relationship pattern with the counsellor which seek to invoke the counsellor's rejection. However, if the counsellor's unconditional positive regard is enduring, the client is faced with the hypothesis that he may be a person of value. This is perhaps the most powerful dissonant element introduced into the client's self-concept. It is also the reason why in person-centred counselling, the *relationship* is said to be the important change agent.

These are three sources of dissonance evoked by person-centred counselling. However, the client is not merely a passive respondent to such dissonance creation. Dissonance evokes a tension – a discomfort which seeks to be reduced perhaps by negating the dissonant elements. The result is that the change processes that are initiated by counselling become accompanied by reactionary forces which seek to reduce the dissonance. The self-concept has begun to fight back to try to reduce the dissonance. Each tentative attempt on the part of the client to bring the self-concept into question is met with a sophisticated barrage of reactionary protective systems. At one level the client would love to change but the organism cannot take the risk to lay aside the familiar and in a sense 'safe' self-concept upon which the whole life is based. Under oppressive conditions of worth the client will have evolved that self-concept as a way of adapting: for the client to risk changing that attitude is, in existential terms, to invite the possibility of his annihilation.

The skill and professionalism of the counsellor is in not being worn down by the client's protective systems because at this stage that protectiveness is much more in evidence than the actualising tendency. Also, the nature of the protectiveness is highly individualised: one client might become very 'stuck' so that the therapeutic process appears to have reached an insurmountable wall, while another might enlarge upon earlier self-defeating behaviour, so that, just when he is developing more autonomous functioning, there is a dramatic reversal into despair: this kind of 'regression' was described in an earlier publication in terms of the client who 'seeks to grasp defeat from the jaws of success' (Mearns, 1992b). The 'stuckness' and regression which is evident during this battle for the self-concept can be difficult for the counsellor to bear. It is easy for the counsellor to become a little disengaged at this period in the process. Of course, any such response is more likely to feed the reactionary forces in the client's self-concept. The counsellor's task is to offer the core conditions consistently to *all* the parts of the client whether they are driven by the actualising tendency or by the reactionary forces – for all these parts have been important to the client's existence past and present. This dialectic between change-orientated forces and reactionary forces is the starting point for the author's revision of Carl Rogers' Self Theory. An early statement is given in chapter 9 of Mearns and Thorne (2000) with a fuller set of propositions summarised in Mearns (2002c).

The great mystery of the therapeutic process is the transition between this struggle within the self-concept and actual self-concept change (see also Zimring, 1990). A prime area for future research is this period late in the middle stage of the counselling process when a significant degree of self-acceptance is won. In clients' reports of their experiences of therapy this change seems to occur in one of two quite different ways which I call *osmotic* and *seismic* change, borrowing these metaphors from biology and geology respectively. In *osmotic* change nothing much seems to make a difference until one day the client realises that everything is different. One client described it thus: 'It feels really strange ... nothing has changed and yet everything is different.' In this form of change it is as though the client has not been aware of the self-concept change which has slowly developed. The process has taken place so gradually that each element of the change was imperceptible, but there has come a time when the client notices the effects of the accumulated change. In this so-called osmotic change the counsellor may have been aware that a change was occurring: she may have perceived the client's re-evaluation of elements of the self-concept and the gradual growth of self-acceptance. Over a period of time she may have seen the client becoming less dominated by old self-protective strategies and gradually finding the freedom to view life situations in new ways. Although the counsellor might have had clear sight of that changing, telling the client what was seen would make little difference. In this form of change process the point at which the change appears to have taken place is merely the point at which the client adopts a changed label for himself or herself; in fact, the change has been progressing for some time. The confusion for the client is that he cannot relate what he perceives as a new change to anything that has recently happened.

At other times the experience of change is more dramatic: the client suddenly makes an enormous shift with respect to his experiencing of an event or his experiencing of himself. The case of 'Joan' (Mearns and Thorne, 1999: chapters 6–8) has examples of this kind of 'sea change' taking place quite dramatically. The best metaphor for this form of change is that it is a *seismic* change: it is as though the pressure towards change has been building up under the surface and then quite suddenly a major shift takes place. This seismic change has its parallels in other examples of attitude change where the attitude maintains itself by its defences through a seemingly huge onslaught, but then quite suddenly changes. For example, the physically abused partner in a relationship may defend against the realisation of the impossibility of that relationship through all sorts of rationalisation and denial until one day he or she 'snaps' and changes his or her attitude for good. At that change point the person is amazed to realise what he or she has tolerated and rationalised in the past. This kind of seismic change is somewhat like a classical conversion experience with the change happening so dramatically that the person may go from one extreme of the attitude to the other. The counsellor should be ready for the *reaction* which can follow seismic change. For instance, the counsellor should not be surprised if the client experiences an apparently *stuck* phase thereafter: the change has been so dramatic that it takes some time to re-orient and rebuild his life. Also, the pendulum may have swung past its optimal balance so that later correction takes place.

> **KEY POINT** This has been one of the largest sections of the book because it is perhaps the most important area for research in person-centred counselling. The therapeutic process is tied to self-concept change, which can create confusing periods of apparent 'stuckness' or even regression.

23 Confronting the client

Western culture is not very sophisticated when it comes to 'confrontation'. We tend to assume that a confrontation is like a battle: a noisy affair with winners and losers. This presumption fits one dictionary definition of confrontation: 'to face in hostility or defiance'. However, other dictionary definitions include 'to bring face to face'/'to compare'/'to juxtapose one view with another'. This latter group of definitions is more reflective of confrontation in person-centred counselling. The most effective confrontations are not even noticed as such, but they have their impact in encouraging the client to compare one construction with another. As described in Section 22, person-centred counselling has the effect of creating or increasing dissonance within the rigid and defended self-concept. Confrontation of different forms stimulates and presents dissonant elements to the self-concept but in a way that is not experienced as threatening, otherwise the self-concept would be more strongly encouraged to exercise its protective functions.

Person-centred counselling is full of confrontation, with the client being challenged to juxtapose one perspective against another; one part of his self alongside another; or a present response contrasted with his long-standing view of himself. These confrontations are offered in the context of a person-centred way of being: in other words, they are founded on the sincere respect which the counsellor feels towards the client, they reflect the counsellor's struggle to understand the client and they are communicated in a way which keeps the client at the centre of his locus of evaluation.

Perhaps the best way to illustrate confrontation in person-centred counselling is to give examples of how it manifests itself within different person-centred procedures.

The most common confronting activity in person-centred counselling is *empathy* (Tscheulin, 1990) where the client is confronted with an accurate reflection of the feelings he has expressed, for example:

Counsellor: So, you feel that you are weak and that if you can't cope like all the other teachers then you are no good and should just get out ... that's how you feel?

Confronting the client with his expression of his feeling implicitly asks several questions simultaneously, including 'Is this *really* how you feel?'; 'Do you in fact feel something else as well?' and 'Have you correctly represented the *intensity* of the feeling?'

Since *focusing* in person-centred counselling (see Section 21) is taken as a special case of empathy, the same applies for the confrontation possibilities of focusing responses. These reflect the client's expressions back to him or her and ask the same kind of questions about their accuracy and their intensity, for example, the word-for-word reflection:

Counsellor: So, you are feeling 'A – bit – let – down'.

The person-centred counsellor is in a *congruent* state of being in relation to the client at all times. Most of the time there is no particular confrontational content in that congruent state of being. However, at times, the different feelings of the counsellor offer confrontation to the client's frame of reference in that moment, for example:

Counsellor: So you want us to stop working together *right now* – this is to be the last session. I find myself feeling two things simultaneously ... one is that I deeply want to respect your wishes and not to push you in any way over this ... the other is that I'm really curious about the rapid change – just last week you were saying how important this work was to you.

This response offers all of the counsellor's feeling in relation to the client's wish to stop the work immediately. The response shows a respect for the client's wishes but also accurately represents the counsellor's curiosity. A confrontational response like this asks the question 'Is there more that we should talk about here?'

The Self Theory underlying person-centred counselling (Rogers, 1951; 1959; Mearns and Thorne, 2000) describes how the process of counselling helps the client to rediscover and *review denied experiences*, juxtaposing these against the self structure to result in a revision of that self structure which becomes more in line with the person's experiencing. The client originates most of these internal confrontations with himself, but occasionally the counsellor proffers the confrontation, for example:

Counsellor: So, you have always regarded yourself as a person who is 'weak' intellectually, and yet, you have just now realised that you were the one who helped others with their work in class?

Similarly, the client will initiate most of the internal confrontations between his sense of himself and the various *introjections* he has swallowed about himself, but occasionally it is the counsellor who voices the confrontation; for example, one client described how he had been moved to tears by warm feedback given to him by a colleague – for one of the few times in his life he had felt that he was 'a good human being'. In relation to this, the counsellor proffers a confrontation between that experience of himself and actual words which the client had previously used to describe his (introjected) view of himself:

Counsellor: So, you are 'an evil person who is poison to anyone who comes close to you'?!

If confrontation is seen in terms of helping the client to hold a mirror to himself in ways which are least likely to encourage defensive reactions, then there is considerable confrontation, in many different forms, within person-centred counselling. However, if confrontation is regarded as an aggressive way of forcing the counsellor's view onto the client then person-centred counselling will have no truck with it. The value of confrontation is in the way it gently invites the client to consider other perspectives and possibilities in such an unobtrusive way that it would not even be experienced as a discontinuity by the client.

> **KEY POINT** There is considerable confrontation in person-centred counselling but it is achieved in a fashion which seeks to keep the client at the centre of his locus of evaluation rather than make the counsellor the centre.

24 Trouble-shooting 'stuckness' within the therapeutic process

'Stuckness' is a hypothetical construct used to denote a state within the therapeutic process when the client does not appear to be moving, preparing for movement or consolidating after movement (Mearns, 1992b).

The issue of 'stuckness' in the therapeutic process was introduced in chapter 7 of *Person-Centred Counselling in Action* (Mearns and Thorne, 1999). The present section seeks to add to the exploration of this multi-faceted phenomenon.

Mearns and Thorne (1999: 154) offer some focusing questions for the counsellor who suspects 'stuckness' in the therapeutic process. Three of these questions provide a framework for 'trouble-shooting' 'stuckness':

1. Are we indeed stuck, or am I misperceiving the process through my own impatience, or perhaps because I expect the client to move in different directions from what is happening just now?
2. How does my *client* perceive the process at this time?
3. If we *are* stuck, what is the source of our 'stuckness'?

The first two questions are important because counsellors frequently perceive 'stuckness' where it does not exist for the client. Usually this is symptomatic of failings in the counsellor's empathy in the sense that the counsellor has not understood the client's process or the client's experience of the counselling process.

When these first two questions are addressed in supervision, or indeed in discussion with the client, many instances of apparent 'stuckness' prove to be simply part of the therapeutic process. The profession of counselling is never more naive than when considering the therapeutic process. The image of a steady and even client 'movement' commencing in the first session and continuing in a straight line through to the end of counselling is particularly evidenced by some counselling agencies that put pressure on their counsellors to terminate if the client has not shown obvious movement during the previous few sessions. This pressure for continuous movement is often created by the stretched resources of the counselling agency which cannot risk the possibility of wasted counselling time when they are faced with considerable need on the waiting list. However, the presumption that steady movement should be the norm manifestly contradicts human experience and may further pathologise the client by inferring that he is not trying, not ready, or for other reasons is wasting the counsellor's time.

The reality of the therapeutic process is that it rarely shows a steady movement and frequently contains some periods when no movement is happening. For example, there is often a period of stillness after the client has made a significant movement. The natural human process at that time is to have a rest, take stock and come to terms with the new reality. There can also be a period of stillness and apparent 'stuckness' *before* a major change happens but this is virtually impossible to identify except retrospectively.

Apparent 'stuckness' and even regression can be a fundamental part of the client's process of self-concept change as exemplified by the self-concept fighting back to reduce the dissonance created by counselling (see Section 22).

If 'stuckness' is diagnosed, question 3 becomes the next trouble-shooting step: what is the *source* of the 'stuckness'? Logically, 'stuckness' in the counselling process can have its source in the *client,* in the *counsellor* or in their *relationship.* Strictly speaking, relationship problems might in turn be traced back to the counsellor and/or the client, but it is useful to retain this tripartite framework because some problems manifest themselves particularly within relationship dynamics.

Client 'stuckness'

Client factors are usually predominant in the various forms of *apparent* 'stuckness' mentioned earlier, but real blocks in the therapeutic process can also result from dynamics within the client's self. An understanding of the Self Theory underpinning the person-centred approach is invaluable for comprehending the many blocks which may stop the client's movement. For example, the client's *denial* mechanisms may be working overtime to counteract the impact of the counselling and the new awarenesses which have resulted. Also, the *introjected* aspects of the client's self structure might contain some particularly firm injunctions against change. The client may come very close to making major movements in his self-concept but then become blocked by a basic introjection. In this way the introjection operates like a pre-programmed security lock to provide a last ditch protection for the self-concept. Two of the most common such devices are the introjections: 'If I consider changing that means I am only fooling myself' and, 'If I begin to feel good about myself that means I am bad and must feel guilty.'

A third important source of client 'stuckness' is where the client's process stops because he fears the potential *losses of change*. The client knows that to proceed will most likely involve life changes that are unacceptable to him, at least at this time. The most common anticipated loss is that which is involved in the break-up of relationships: the client sees himself moving further and faster away from the primary relationship and checks his movement through fear of that loss.

Sometimes client stuckness, in any of the above forms, can be understood in terms of *Configuration Theory* (see Section 4; Mearns, 1999; Mearns and Thorne, 2000; Mearns, 2002c). The client may symbolise two or more parts or 'configurations' of his self that carry opposing imperatives and, in effect, cancel each other out, for example: 'Part of me wants to leave this relationship' and 'part of me does not'. For the counsellor to 'focus on the stuckness' between these imperatives is largely a waste of time – stuckness is a dynamic and does not focus. It is more effective to regard both of these two parts as clients and afford the therapeutic relationship to each in turn. Each of these parts will have considerable life though the two together might represent a 'zero sum' (Mearns and Thorne, 2000: chapter 7). Focusing on the 'part of me that wants to leave this relationship' could reveal all sorts of dimensions and might lead to new realisations. But, since both of these parts represent our client, a discipline is required also to focus upon 'the part of me that does not want to leave this relationship' to explore where that will lead. In this way, the counsellor does not simply 'stay with stuckness' but relates with the parts of the client involved in the stuckness dynamic.

Counsellor 'stuckness'

To presume that 'stuckness' in the therapeutic process can arise only as a result of client factors is to ignore the fact that there are two people in the room. The therapeutic process may become stuck through the influence of the counsellor's *values*, *fears* or deep-seated *needs*. Thankfully, one of the results of the growth of professional levels of training for counselling is that many of the potential roots of counsellor 'stuckness' are uncovered and addressed during training as in the case of the examples which follow.

The counsellor who has strongly held *values* that become imposed upon the client creates new 'conditions of worth' for the client. Instead of finding freedom from such conditions of worth, the client experiences messages such as: 'I am valued when: I am weak/I am strong/I talk in terms of staying with my wife rather than leaving her/I don't question the counsellor's view/I keep having peak experiences in counselling'. In some cases the client may be *presuming* these conditions where they are not in fact being portrayed by the counsellor but in other situations these conditions of worth will be real in the sense that they are actually reflecting values which are being manifested through the counsellor's behaviour. With a vulnerable client these counsellor imposed conditions of worth will further alienate the client from his self and from his locus of evaluation, and with a client who is not so vulnerable the therapeutic process will terminate or become stuck.

The counsellor's *fear* may create 'stuckness' in the therapeutic process. One form of this is where the counsellor comes up against a *wall* within herself in relation to the fear and despair which the client is experiencing. Counsellors do not need to have experienced everything that their clients have experienced, but it is undoubtedly a help if, at some time in their lives, they have plumbed their own existential depths or they may become personally fearful when working at that level with clients. At times the wall which the counsellor comes up against has to do with incomplete transitions in her own life. It is difficult to work with a client on a transition where the counsellor is personally stuck because that tends to induce fear on the part of the counsellor. When the counsellor is fearful she will tend to behave in ways which arrest the therapeutic process.

A much more disturbing category of counsellor 'stuckness' is where the counsellor's deep-seated *needs* become involved in the therapeutic process with the client. Here we could exemplify a whole range of needs which can become 'over involved' in the process, for example: a need to create client dependency; an excessive need for affection; a need to be admired, or a need to control. Any of these and many other deep-seated needs in the counsellor can constrain the relationship and the therapeutic process into one which serves the needs of the counsellor before those of the client. In this circumstance one way in which the client is protected from damage is for the process to become stuck.

Relationship 'stuckness'

Section 17 explored the unspoken relationship between client and counsellor pointing out that if the relationship is neglected the unspoken assumptions and restrictive norms can build up to the extent that the therapeutic relationship becomes smothered. Counsellors who have difficulty in being fully 'present' in the relationship are particularly prone to this form of relationship 'stuckness': their relationships start well enough but do not develop beyond a certain level of immediacy and intimacy. As was mentioned earlier, this might be categorised as 'stuckness' emanating from the counsellor, but it manifests itself in the relationship dynamics.

Another variety of relationship 'stuckness' occurs where one part of the personality of the counsellor becomes enmeshed with a part of the client's personality. In the demanding interpersonal contexts created during training the counsellor will have become aware of many of these inter-actional difficulties but others may arise even after many years' experience, as in the example quoted in Mearns and Dryden (1989: 95).

> The client and I got down into a very deep level of work and then found that somehow her deepest self had some kind of antagonism or experience of threat from my deepest self. I went to my own therapist saying that I felt really despairing about it and unable to continue. I felt as if I were touching bottom. If there was this deep rift, how could the therapy continue.

This counsellor worked his way out of the 'stuckness' by raising and exploring the issue with his client so that they could both fight for the relationship. As a general strategy the open exploration of the 'stuckness' with the client affords appropriate respect to the client as a partner in the endeavour.

The exploration of the 'stuckness' is important because of the potentially important therapeutic material which underlies client 'stuckness' and relationship 'stuckness'. Of course, there is also much to be learned in the case of counsellor 'stuckness'. The counsellor may try to do that learning through supervision of audiotapes but sometimes it can only be uncovered in open exploration with the client. This raises the question of the counsellor's courage and commitment to the client.

> **KEY POINT**   Although 'stuckness' is a phenomenon which may be feared by counsellors, the challenge is to understand and to work with the experience.

V

Person-Centred
Psychopathology

25 The person-centred perspective on psychopathology: the neurotic client

ELKE LAMBERS

Introduction

Person-centred theory is sometimes criticised for not giving enough attention to the development of psychopathology and to the specific issues arising from it in therapy. Indeed, person-centred counselling does not prescribe specific treatments for different disorders and it has avoided the use of diagnostic language. The person-centred counsellor endeavours to understand the specific conflicts of the individual client rather than to see the client as representing a broader category (Mearns, 1997a: 143).

Person-centred counselling has much to offer in the mental health field, but in order to develop its potential in this important area of practice it is imperative that counsellors seek to articulate with the language and the frame of reference of psychiatry and mental health. This does not mean that the medical diagnostic system has to be adopted, but rather that the counsellor learns to understand that language and is able to communicate coherently her person-centred conceptualisation of the client's difficulties.

This section of the book offers an introduction to how counsellors can conceptualise psychopathology in a way that does not compromise the basic values of the person-centred approach. A first step is look at the concept of diagnosis.

Diagnosis

The conventional dictionary definition of 'diagnosis' is that it is an identification of a disease from an examination of its symptoms. Translating this medical language into the psychological realm would give us something like 'identification of a problem from an examination of the behaviour and experience of the person'. This is not so different from what goes on in the client during the therapeutic process. Indeed Rogers makes the same observation:

> Therapy is basically the experiencing of the inadequacies in old ways of perceiving, the experiencing of new and more accurate perceptions, and the recognition of significant relationships between perceptions. In a very meaningful sense, therapy *is* diagnosis, and this diagnosis is a process which goes on in the experience of the client, rather than in the intellect of the therapist. It is in this way that the client-centered therapist has confidence in the efficacy of the diagnosis. (Rogers, 1951: 222–3)

Indeed, the counsellor joins in with this diagnostic process. She sees how the client perceives himself and his world and how he links past events with present circumstances and future aspirations. The process of counselling is one by which the client evolves his own diagnostic theory about himself, aided by the counsellor providing the relationship which helps him to feel safe enough to stay open to his experiencing. From this person-centred perspective diagnosis is a thoroughly individualised process with results which are unique for each client. It is also a process by which both client and counsellor stay open to the client's experience (Mearns, 1997a: 146).

This concept of diagnosis is quite different from that which is associated with the medical world where diagnosis is an assessment of the patient by the practitioner. The assessment is not particularly individualised but is directed into categories, essentially because treatment plans have been derived for work with the various diagnostic categories. Of course, this concept of diagnosis is seriously at odds with person-centred counselling which does not relate 'treatment' to specific categories or problems. Instead, person-centred counselling is characterised by its focus on the relationship between client and counsellor. The person-centred counsellor is committed to the client as primary reference point and rejects the pursuit of control or authority over the client (Bozarth and Temaner Brodley, 1986). Rogers describes diagnosis as in direct conflict with this basic philosophy and as potentially detrimental to the therapeutic relationship. Diagnosis implicitly places the locus of evaluation outside the client and makes the counsellor into an expert who consequently may determine the direction and goal of the therapeutic work (Rogers, 1951). After the Wisconsin project, which explored the extent to which hospitalised chronic schizophrenic patients could benefit from client-centred counselling he concluded that 'regardless of whether we are working with psychotics, normal delinquents or neurotics, the most essential ingredients for therapeutic change are in the quality of the relationship' (Rogers et al., 1967: 92). Diagnosis is therefore irrelevant to the therapeutic process.

The discussion about the value and danger of diagnosis has continued since then. Those against any form of diagnosis assert that psychodiagnosis is inaccurate and that it cannot possibly capture the complexity of a person's essence and inner world (Boy, 1989: 137); that it does not take into account the social and cultural context (Patel and Winston, 1994); and that it emphasises what is 'pathological' rather than what is healthy (Kottler and Brown, 1985). Diagnosis ultimately reduces the person to a label.

While the person-centred approach might take a completely different approach to the notion of 'diagnosis' that does not mean that we are exempted from developing an understanding of the language of others in this regard. It will be to the benefit of our clients if we can articulate with other mental health workers. Hence, it is important to know the conventional meanings of psychodiagnostic labels. But, we can go even further than this. We can consider how person-centred theory would approach the descriptions of people given in the psychodiagnostic categories. This takes us into person-centred psychopathology.

Person-centred psychopathology

In his personality theory Rogers describes the development of psychological maladjustment and disorganisation as a theoretical formulation that applies to every individual to a greater or lesser degree (Rogers, 1959: 228).

Central to his theory is the incongruence between self and experience – that what we call our 'self' can become skewed from the actual experiences we have had of our 'self'. This effect is created by the 'conditions of worth' we have had to negotiate. External 'authorities' (parents, partners, cultural values, religions, etc.) will have had certain expectations for us and we will have tried to internalise these ways of being in order to maintain our attachment. Equally, we will have had to deny or distort our experiences of our self that run counter to the way we are 'supposed' to be. Hence, we begin to believe we are what we are not and to deny what we are. This is the essential 'incongruence' Rogers talks about. The extent to which the incongruence induces 'disturbance' in us will depend on many factors, including:

- The nature of the conditions of worth.
- The degree of incongruence.
- The difficulty we have in maintaining a reasonably consistent image of ourself in the face of this incongruence.
- The nature of the protections we erect in an effort to maintain that consistent image.

Rogers' view of disturbance is that it is a *process* rather than a condition or a rigid state. Since the disturbance is as a result of our efforts to negotiate the incongruence and those negotiations will change with our life circumstances, so will our disturbance follow an evolving process.

This is a very brief account of Rogers' basic concept of psychopathology. There are many other concepts and processes which could be described. In these four sections we will look at the most common diagnostic categories indicating what they look like with respect to the client's experience and how they might be understood in terms of person-centred theory.

Presenting symptoms of neurosis

The client expresses feelings of inadequacy, unhappiness and dissatisfaction. He does not know himself, nor does he understand himself. His relationships are not satisfactory and there is a sense of not getting anywhere, of being stuck. Life is a struggle; it is difficult to make decisions; there are doubts, fears, anxieties, feelings of guilt and sometimes also persistent physical symptoms and complaints for which no organic basis can be found. He may be preoccupied with specific worries which dominate his life and which become a regular, if not the only, focus for the counselling sessions. Headaches, anxiety symptoms, health worries, concern about a child, a partner, a decision, anything can be presented as 'the problem', leaving the counsellor struggling to make contact with the client beyond the level of such concerns. When the client has difficulties with making decisions, he seeks advice and guidance from others, including the counsellor, but cannot act on any advice he may get. He communicates his feelings in an incongruent way, has difficulties with expressing himself clearly and is over-concerned with the opinions people have of him. He tries to please everyone and does not seem to know what he wants or needs for himself. He hopes the counsellor can help him to feel better and at the same time worries that she will get fed up with him. He might be represented by Matthew in Box 25.1.

Box 25.1

Undoing the conditions of worth

Matthew: I sometimes just feel sorry for myself. Why can't I be more like my brother, more outgoing and confident, more liked. I wonder if things will ever be different . . .

Therapist: You can get really low sometimes – feeling miserable, envious and hopeless . . .

Matthew: You are right. I should pull myself together. It's not right that I should be envious of my brother. I am sorry . . . I should not moan so much. You want to hear something positive for a change.

Therapist: Matthew, I really hear how difficult things are for you just now. Like you can't get it right anywhere. And you are worried about what I might think of you . . .

Matthew: [*tears in his eyes*] I just hate feeling this way – it scares me that you might get fed up with me. But yes, I sometimes just can't stand my brother . . .

Person-centred conceptualisation of neurosis

Strong conditions of worth were, or still are, present in the client's important relationships. They were probably fairly clear and consistent, relating to the expression of particular feelings and to specific behaviour. Punishment for not conforming to the conditions of worth took the form of *withdrawal of affection and acceptance*, causing feelings of self-hate, inadequacy, unworthiness, fear of rejection and guilt. Self-expression has become limited and is controlled by the conditions of worth. The self-concept is rigid and negative, maintained with the help of powerful defence mechanisms. Unacceptable feelings are denied or distorted, both to avoid rejection by others and to avoid the unbearable awareness of inner conflict. The more disturbed the person, the more difficult it will be for him to believe anything about himself or to trust himself and the more incongruent he will be. The locus of evaluation is outside the self:

as the person cannot be fully open to his experience and gets more and more out of touch with the self he finds it hard to know his feelings and to express these congruently. He relies on others for an evaluation of his feelings as 'right' or 'wrong'. He seeks guidance and approval and is unable to make decisions or act on his own feelings. The client is in a state of *incongruence*: he is out of touch with the experience of the self, has difficulties with self-acceptance and does not feel able to be 'real'. He may have an explanation for the way he is: his personal story which explains his self-concept, his symptoms and the reason for his stuckness or his inability to make decisions or to change (Swildens, 1990).

Issues in the therapeutic relationship with a neurotic client

In the therapeutic relationship issues of *trust, power* and *dependency* are likely to be around. The client may be anxious to be seen as a 'good' client and invests the counsellor with a great deal of power: the power of the expert, of the person who knows him better than he knows himself, the person who can give advice and direction and who has the power to judge him. He will be very sensitive to conditions of worth in the therapeutic relationship, always ready to fit into these where they exist or are imagined. Faced with such a client the counsellor may feel under pressure to perform, to be an expert, or to rescue the client, especially when an impasse in the therapeutic process is reached. The client who has his locus of evaluation outside himself attributes power to those around him and the counsellor who is not sufficiently aware of this kind of pressure – and of her own response to it – may find herself in a relationship where *both* counsellor and client experience feelings of dependency, responsibility for the other person and guilt about not being good enough. Therapeutic change is most likely to take place where the counsellor is able to create the conditions that can lead to greater congruence, self-acceptance and openness to self-experience in the client. The counsellor's empathic understanding and responding not only help the client to feel understood and valued but it also helps him to listen to himself, to begin to hear himself and so open himself up to his own experiencing. Unconditional positive regard, acceptance of the client as he is and not as he can be, creates a relationship where he is unburdened from the conditions of worth that have been such a feature of his development and where his self acceptance is allowed to grow. The counsellor's congruence and realness in the relationship offer the client a different model of a way of being, facilitating the development of his own congruence.

Working with a client who is gradually becoming more congruent, increasingly willing to take risks and to make decisions, is tremendously moving and rewarding for the counsellor. Yet this necessary and legitimate satisfaction can become the source of over-involvement and conditionality if the client has to live up to the counsellor's expectations and needs. Needless to say, the neurotic counsellor is particularly vulnerable to inducing such conditionality.

> **KEY POINT** Historically, person-centred counselling has resisted diagnostic labels lest they obstruct our view of the individuality of the client. However, it is possible to understand, for example, neurosis in terms of person-centred theory. Such an analysis may help the counsellor to understand her own responses to the neurotic client.

26 Borderline personality disorder

ELKE LAMBERS

Presenting symptoms of borderline personality disorder

The person with borderline personality disorder may present a wide variety of symptoms, such as impulsive behaviour, self-harm, mood swings, chronic feelings of emptiness and boredom (American Psychiatric Association, 1987). She may have psychotic experiences and paranoid reactions, usually of a temporary nature. The person's life may appear chaotic with destructive and damaging relationships, engagement in 'dangerous' behaviour such as substance abuse, promiscuity and criminal acts. She may have a tendency to over-indulge, for instance in eating, sexual behaviour or gambling. Sometimes there are feelings of depersonalisation, anxiety attacks and a slipping in and out of altered states of consciousness. In times of acute disturbance the person may have been admitted to hospital, indeed the borderline client often commutes between hospital and community settings (Swildens, 1990). People with borderline personality disorder are not disturbed all the time; there are periods when they do not act 'borderline' (Kroll, 1988) and in some important areas they appear to function without great difficulty (Swildens, 1991). Some researchers suggest that 30 per cent to 70 per cent of all psychotherapy clients fall into this group (Rohde-Dachser, 1979).

Person-centred conceptualisation of borderline personality disorder

Inconsistency in conditions of worth, lack of validation of experience, abuse and emotional neglect may contribute to the development of the vulnerable, unstable self-concept of the client with borderline personality disorder. Her experience has constantly been ignored, denied, criticised or violated and as a consequence she has not been able to develop a self-concept which is informed by her experience. Instead, her sense of self is derived from the definition others give to her experience. As a result she cannot rely on her inner experience as a guide to action, she has no coherent base for response and instead she has to take cues for her response from the immediate situation (Bohart, 1990: 613). She has not learned to listen to or to trust her experience and this inability to focus makes it difficult to deal with situations where she has to create meaning (Bohart, 1990). Her self-concept lacks boundaries, consistency, continuity and protection; it is constantly under threat as it has no effective means of evaluating and integrating new experiences (Swildens, 1990: 627). She may experience *fragile process*, finding it difficult to hold experience in attention to a moderate level, resulting in either being overwhelmed or finding it extremely difficult to make contact with experience (Warner, 2001: 182).

In some cases the fragility of the self-concept may be the consequence of extremely powerful traumatic experiences which cannot be integrated in the self-concept nor be distorted or denied. Although such an undeniable experience may be kept from awareness through, for example, repression or dissociation, it remains a dissonant element in the experience of the self. If such an experience occurs in later life it can cause emotional breakdown; if it takes place earlier in the development of the self-concept it may result in a fragmented, chaotic self. Warner describes this as *dissociated process*, where, as a defence against the experience of severe trauma the person develops the ability to move into trance-like states and clusters of dissociated experiences may develop a distinctive, person-like nature often referred to as 'parts' (Warner, 2000; 161).

In the absence of consistent and reliable protection of the self the client with borderline personality reacts to threat in whatever manner seems most likely to ensure survival. Defences such as distortion, projection, denial and splitting, are all deployed to protect the fragile self-concept, resulting in disturbed, unpredictable, chaotic behaviour (Swildens, 1990). However, these defensive responses occur only in situations where the self is threatened by new experiences. In the absence of such threat the client can function well (Bohart, 1990; Swildens, 1990).

Issues in the therapeutic relationship with a client with borderline personality disorder

The counselling relationship, with its closeness and its focus on the self of the client, is potentially very threatening to someone with an unstable, vulnerable self-concept. The new experiencing of the self which is part of the process of therapeutic change is dangerous. Where there is so much fear around, the counsellor needs to offer the client a relationship where she can feel safe, valued, respected and understood in her struggle to survive. The client's fear of closeness to others and to her own experiencing needs to be respected and this may mean that the counsellor has to refrain from what would be experienced as intrusive forms of empathic responding and challenging of the client's defences. The therapist's response has to be finely tuned to reflect the client's experience with exactness and sensitivity to her emotional vulnerability (Warner, 2000; 2001).

The client's disturbed behaviour may be challenging and threatening for the counsellor. The counsellor's congruent awareness of herself in the relationship is of great importance in order to avoid becoming involved in unhelpful conflict which will only threaten the client further. In order to be able to develop a firmer, more stable self-concept the client needs the security of a relationship where the counsellor knows how to be present and at the same time can keep her distance. It is important that the client's attempts at making sense of *both* her internal and external reality are supported. In practice this could mean not only attending to the client's inner experience but also supporting her in her efforts to cope with the demands of her life (Swildens, 1990; Van de Veire, 1995). The fact that the client has a chaotic personality can make relating with her a chaotic experience for the counsellor. Box 26.1 illustrates this by reproducing a portion of the counsellor's notes.

Box 26. 1

Relating with a client with borderline process can be a chaotic experience

Counsellor's notes: Tuesday

I am wondering what is happening with Sylvia. We got on really well in our first six sessions, but now she is different. I really thought we were getting somewhere – she brought me poems and drawings about how she was feeling and she was really keen to explore things. But in the last few sessions she has become difficult – she arrives either too late or too early, she avoids looking at me and she seems angry. Last week I wondered if she had been drinking. At the end of that session she did not want to make an appointment, but later that day she phoned me in tears and apologised. I am finding it hard going; I sometimes feel annoyed at her, but when I think about it a bit more I can see that she seems really scared and lost. How can I let her know that I understand her without frightening her even more . . .

KEY POINT   The counselling relationship is potentially threatening for the fragile self-concept of the client with borderline personality disorder. The counsellor needs to communicate her empathic understanding and respect for the client's struggle to survive, offering a secure relationship in which the client may develop a firmer, more stable sense of herself.

27 Psychosis

ELKE LAMBERS

Presenting symptoms of psychotic process

It is important to note that this concept is not in itself a diagnostic category, nor does it refer only to the specific condition known as 'schizophrenia'. The term psychosis is used to describe a psychological process in which the person is withdrawn from normal contact, is experiencing reality in a distorted way and is unable to communicate clearly with others. His behaviour may be bizarre or inappropriate; speech and affect may be disturbed; there are sometimes delusions, hallucinations, strange thought patterns and disorientation with memory loss. This state of mind can be present in association with other forms of disturbance, or it may be an isolated temporary condition. It is not unusual for someone who is depressed to go through a psychotic episode, or to find psychotic behaviour in someone with an elated manic mood. Withdrawal from drugs and certain organic conditions can also produce psychotic symptoms.

Person-centred conceptualisation of psychotic process

Rogers describes psychosis as a state of disintegration, involving the breakdown of the neurotic defences of denial and distortion and the development of extreme forms of defence such as paranoid and catatonic behaviour (Rogers, 1959: 228). The self is protected by what seems an impenetrable, rigid shield. The person is unable to be reached and can communicate only in what seems to be a coded language. In a psychotic style of processing the person has difficulty with expressing their experience in a way that makes sense within the culture, or which offers a predictive value in relation to their environment (Warner, 2001: 183). He has withdrawn from the reality which is shared with others. One of the basic needs for survival, the need for valuing and acceptance, cannot be met. This results in profound isolation and diminished social functioning. The threat to the self must be enormous for this kind of catastrophic response to take place.

Issues in the therapeutic relationship with a psychotic client

It is important not to over-react to the presence of strange behaviour, bizarre thought patterns or unusual use of language. Such symptoms can alert the counsellor to the possibility of a psychotic disorder, but there may be other ways of understanding them. The counsellor has to listen very carefully, taking into account her own view of reality, the client's cultural context and the client's personal language. What can seem a bizarre thought may turn out to be a metaphor. Incoherence, confusion or emotional turmoil may be an understandable response to a crisis situation. What sounds like a delusion or a paranoid thought may prove to have some basis in reality.

In Sections 29 and 30 on 'pre-therapy', Van Werde describes in detail the approach for establishing psychological contact with the psychotic client. I shall therefore limit myself to general comments on therapeutic issues with this client group. Working with a client in psychosis is very demanding upon the counsellor's ability to create the therapeutic conditions and a fundamental challenge to the therapist's understanding and expression of the conditions. Being with someone whose communication is designed to be both understood and not understood, the counsellor will have to find her own, idiosyncratic, way of expressing her empathic understanding. Acceptance of the psychotic experience is essential. This does not mean that the therapist adopts the client's reality, but that she accepts the reality as it is for the client and that she has no need or wish to change it or to distance herself from it (Berghofer, 1996: 490). At the same time, she has to be clear and honest with herself, accepting that she has boundaries and limits and working within those. Congruence, both within the counsellor and in her communication with the client, is essential. People suffering from psychosis are particularly skilled at recognising incongruence and only if the conditions are optimal will the client take the risk of exploring those carefully guarded experiences (Van Werde, 1998: 198). When faced with a confused and confusing client, the counsellor needs to be in touch with her own inner reality – after all, that may be the only thing of which she can be sure and once some trust has been established it may be the first thing about which the client can be sure. In Box 27.1, a counsellor who is new to work with this clientele gives us a glimpse of her difficulty.

Box 27.1

Working with a psychotic client

Counsellor's notes: Wednesday

Being with Mark took a lot out of me today. He looked scared, did not want to sit down, he stood by the door as if ready to run. I did not know what to do – whether to sit down, stand beside him, or how close to stand to him. He kept repeating that his head hurt from hitting it against a wall and he kept asking what time it was. I felt clumsy, self-conscious, scared too. I lost track of time – the hour seemed to last forever. I began to feel a bit unreal, a bit crazy . . .

In addition to the three core conditions, the concept of a fourth condition, 'sufficiency of the therapeutic context' (Mearns, 1989) seems particularly relevant. The psychotic client will most likely require a different therapeutic context than the neurotic client. A weekly meeting in a consulting room with a psychotic client is not likely to be a sufficient context for client and counsellor to get to know each other and for trust to develop. The therapeutic hour, so convenient for work with neurotic clients who are willing and able to fit into the counsellor's structure, may be too long or not long enough for the psychotic client. The client may also require a 'holding' environment where his physical needs and safety are secured. Unfortunately, in our culture there is very little variety of holding environments on offer beyond hospitals. Given a therapeutic context which includes perhaps daily meetings between counsellor and client within a holding environment where the counsellor has a comprehensive understanding and ability to create the therapeutic conditions and is secure and supported in herself, then that counselling may be more meaningfully assessed and compared with other treatments. The therapeutic context is a crucial variable in work with the psychotic client.

The person-centred philosophy, with its positive view of human nature and its belief in the self-actualising tendency, can induce in the counsellor a false sense of confidence and optimism. 'Rescuer' fantasies, fascination with the client's inner world, the challenge and excitement of working with difficult clients can all lead to a situation where the counsellor is in fact working beyond her limits, is out of her depth and not safe. Working with deeply disturbed clients is demanding, challenging and requires a great deal of commitment and responsibility. It also requires skill, depth, a certain amount of knowledge and understanding, as well as acceptance of limitations. In the long run it could be better *not* to take on a client if there is any doubt about support for the client in the world outside the therapy room, or if the counsellor is not sufficiently confident about her ability to offer a safe therapeutic relationship.

> **KEY POINT** Working with a client in psychosis is a fundamental challenge to the counsellor's ability to offer the core conditions. Therapeutic context is a critical variable.

28 Personality disorder

ELKE LAMBERS

Presenting symptoms of personality disorder

The *Training Guide* of the American Psychiatric Association's *Diagnostic Statistical Manual* of mental disorders (Reid and Wise, 1989) describes the category of personality disorder in terms of chronic maladaptive personality characteristics causing subjective distress or significant impairment of the person's ability to function as a social being. These characteristics represent enduring patterns of perceiving, relating to and thinking about oneself and the environment. They are characteristic of both recent as well as long-term functioning and must have been present at least since early adulthood.

Clients with a personality disorder may express feelings of dissatisfaction with their functioning or their relationships, but they do not complain of a 'disorder' in itself. They see their unhappiness or dissatisfaction as being caused by 'things going wrong' in their life: a failure of some sort, losing a job, the ending of a relationship, a threat to an existing way of life, or recurring difficulties in relationships. The cause for such threats is perceived as located in others outside the client and outwith his control. The best-known representative of this group is probably the anti-social personality (psychopath): the person who is preoccupied with his own interests, mercenary in his attitude, manipulative, aggressive and with a tendency for anti-social, possibly criminal behaviour. However, there are many other ways in which a disordered personality can manifest itself. Clients in this category can appear self-absorbed, over-emotional, erratic, suspicious and irritable. They may complain of anxiety symptoms and feelings of depression. A feature which all clients with personality disorder seem to have in common is their persistent difficulty in establishing and maintaining mutually satisfying relationships in adult life.

Person-centred conceptualisation of personality disorder

Significant relationships in the client's early life have been characterised by neglect or persistent abuse of power, expressed in various forms of emotional, physical or sexual abuse, sometimes combinations of all three. The environment has been emotionally and possibly physically very unsafe. Conditions of worth have been linked with satisfying the needs of those with the power: 'you shall satisfy my needs whatever they may be and whenever I want. If you don't, you will be hurt and you will deserve it ...' Refusal or inability to comply would have resulted in anger, punishment and abuse. Compliance may have been met with rewards of presents, privileges, affection and short-lived attention. However, there would have been no predictability or reliability in the environment – what was good one day may have been bad the next. As a consequence the client learned only to live in the moment and is not able to learn from his experience.

His sense of self is determined by how others treat him and he can see the consequences of his behaviour only in terms of the consequences for himself. He is essentially 'ego syntonic': everything is evaluated and perceived in the framework of his own experiences and feelings. He is not able to empathise with others, to see the perspective of others, nor can he be open to non-defensive reflection on his own experiencing.

His self-concept, developed in an environment where the basic need for survival of the organism – the need to be valued – is consistently not met, has at its core a profound sense of worthlessness. To bring this core sense of worthlessness into awareness would be very dangerous. When there is a threat of being faced with that worthlessness the person protects himself by projecting blame for his pain onto others. The client cannot acknowledge the experience of inner conflict – he *can* acknowledge the pain and frustration of being hurt or misunderstood.

In childhood and adolescence this protective system may have helped the person to survive, albeit in a way which may be perceived by others as somewhat 'unthinking', 'selfish' or even 'delinquent'. However, in adulthood the 'protections' of not reflecting on his or her own experience, not empathising and also projecting the blame for his difficulties onto others, become severely dysfunctional. This person does not have the skills to experience trust, intimacy and mutuality with others. The person may enter counselling but, since he does not locate the source of his difficulties within himself, he may feel that he has been forced to seek help and consequently his motivation for sustained therapeutic work may be limited.

Issues in the therapeutic relationship with the personality disordered client

In the therapeutic relationship power, trust and security are likely to be important issues. The client needs to feel secure and the counsellor's clarity and honesty about boundaries, commitment, rules and expectations in the therapeutic relationship are important for his own and the client's security.

The client who feels basically worthless, unloved, unable to love and unaccepted will recreate patterns of relationship where these feelings are confirmed and this constitutes a major challenge for the counsellor. Anger, rejection, seduction and hostility may be used as defences against growing intimacy.

Empathic understanding may not come easily for the counsellor. The client's experiences may be difficult to track when they are apparently superficial, or sometimes extreme. Also, the client who does not reflect on his own experiencing may not be able to perceive the counsellor's empathy: the experience of empathy is totally alien to him. To accept a client whose way of being may be threatening or challenging, both outwith and within the therapeutic relationship, is not easy and is impossible without a degree of empathic understanding of the client in his world.

Being real in the relationship can feel very dangerous for the counsellor. To be transparent may make her feel vulnerable and open to attack or rejection. In her wish to be congruently present she may find herself getting involved in the client's usual pattern of relationship, where either one can be abused or be the abuser, a victim or attacker. Staying in the relationship may be a real struggle, with the counsellor steering a difficult course between the wish to remain accepting and fully present and the need to protect herself. Where the counsellor is not sufficiently aware of her own vulnerabilities and unresolved personal issues she is in danger of becoming either over-involved or under-involved.

Therapeutic change is perhaps most likely to take place through the client's experience of the *consistency* and *durability* of the counsellor's empathic acceptance, giving him the experience of being worthwhile. The counsellor's open, non-abusive presence may give him a novel experience of himself in a relationship, creating a different awareness of himself and of others. Rather than repair or undo the early profound damage to the self, this may help him to create more satisfying relationships and to use his own resources in what is for him a more constructive way. Box 28.1 is an account given by 'Sandy' of his experience some 25 years earlier as a patient in Bruno Bettelheim's Orthogenic School in Chicago. Sandy gives a unique insight into both the promise and the threat offered by therapeutic help. It is no wonder that this kind of client is cautious.

Box 28. 1

'Sandy'

The fellow who has a parent who is sometimes nice and sometimes horrible thinks that is the way the world is. Now, in my own case, that is how it was. At the time when I came to the school I think the difficulty was, among other things, that I was confronted by Patti [his counsellor], who was an exceptionally fine human being and a very affectionate and decent human being. I wasn't able to accept the affection, which caused even more anger because everyone likes to accept affection. But if you condition yourself to not accepting affection because, if by accepting it you only let yourself in for the next downfall, you put yourself in a position where by accepting it you are asking for your own destruction. So, you find yourself in a position where you don't dare to hope that the affection is for real and you keep *testing* to find out if it is for real, and that's the process where, step by step, you find out whether it is. In a sense, maybe, that explains my own need to hurt those who had been kind, because I needed to find out if I hurt them, whether or not the affection would continue to come ... (Bettelheim, 1987)

No matter how we explain our clients' difficulties, the most important thing a person-centred counsellor can offer is her willingness to accept the client first and foremost as a person who is struggling to make sense out of his life, to live with paradoxes and to survive. In that struggle he may have become difficult to understand, fearful, distrusting, defensive, unpredictable and inaccessible. It is the task of the counsellor to accept and respect the client as he is, to find a way of making meaningful contact that leaves the client his value and gives him the option to make a kind of contact that is different from that to which he is accustomed. If clients come away from such a relationship with a bit more hope, a bit more faith in themselves and in others, then that is a considerable influence upon their lives. See the work with the client 'Bobby' in Mearns and Thorne (2000: chapter 3) for an illustration of the challenges posed by this kind of client.

> **KEY POINT** At the core of the self-concept of the client with personality disorder is a profound sense of worthlessness. A central issue in the counselling relationship is acceptance. The counsellor is likely to experience challenge of her ability to offer acceptance; the client will be challenged in his ability to experience being accepted .

29 An introduction to client-centred pre-therapy

DION VAN WERDE

Garry Prouty's 'pre-therapy' (Prouty, 1976; 1994; Prouty, Van Werde and Pörtner (forthcoming)) is well suited as a source of inspiration and a departure point for highly concrete client-therapist interaction.

Pre-therapy is a client-centred theory and methodology designed for work with clients whose ability to establish and maintain *contact is* impaired. 'Contact' is a broad concept encompassing the client's ability to make contact with *reality,* with *other people* and with his own *affective self.* Pre-therapy has been documented and applied to mentally retarded populations (Prouty, 1976; Van Werde, 1990; Peters, 1999), acute psychosis (Van Werde, 1989), chronic schizophrenics (Prouty, 1994), people with multiple personality (Roy, 1991), trauma (Coffeng, 1996) and crisis intervention (Prouty and Kubiak, 1988). The idea of *contact* has also been used as a conceptual framework for ward-setting in residential care for psychotic people (Van Werde 1992; 1998). Pre-therapy has also been described in regard to working with a child in a home-situation (McWilliams and Prouty, 1998) and with people suffering from dementia (Van Werde and Morton, 1999; Van Werde, 2002).

The core idea of the approach and of its applications with various client populations and different settings is that *contact is* the necessary condition for a therapeutic relationship. In his famous 1957 article, Carl Rogers stated the six necessary and sufficient conditions for therapeutic personality change to occur. The conditions which relate to empathy, congruence and unconditional positive regard are well known but the original contribution which Prouty has made to person-centred theory and practice is to underline the importance and expand on the first condition as formulated by Rogers: 'it is necessary that two persons are in psychological contact' (Rogers, 1957: 96).

Prouty works with clients whose communication is severely impaired for various reasons. In work with such clients even a minimal degree of contact cannot be presupposed as it can in work with less impaired clients. Finding a relative vacuum in person-centred theory and practice, Prouty tried to develop client-centred therapy in this area. His initial article, published in 1976, gave the start to an exciting journey of research and practice that is summarised in his first book entitled *Theoretical Evolutions in Person-Centered/Experiential Therapy* (Prouty, 1994). His second book (Prouty, Van Werde and Pörtner, forthcoming) examines the translation of pre-therapy into a ward-milieu and gives an overview of existing pre-therapy projects in Europe.

Pre-therapy centres on the notion of the client developing psychological contact with the World, Self and Other (Merleau-Ponty, 1962). Contact is theoretically described on three levels. First, it is a set of therapeutic reflections by which the therapist makes contact with the client. These reflections take five different forms but all are intended to make contact with the client by reflecting back concrete client behaviour and/or relevant elements from the surrounding reality. Throughout its applications person-centred therapy aims to meet the client at the level of the client's experiencing. With the clientele for which pre-therapy is designed, that level of experiencing must be very basic as indicated by the five forms of *contact reflections*. In *Situational Reflections* (SR), people, places, things and events are reflected, for example 'The sun is shining', 'We are in my office'. These reflections are intended to restore or strengthen the client's contact with his immediate environment. *Facial Reflections* (FR) reflect the concrete features of the emotion that is implicitly present on the face of the client, for example 'You smile', 'Peter looks angry'. The purpose of such reflections is to assist the client to contact and express pre-expressive feeling. In *Body Reflections* (BR), the client's movements or body postures are reflected by means of words or by empathically mirroring them, for example, 'Your arm is up'; or perhaps the therapist rocks in his seat in the same manner as the client. These reflections assist the client to develop an immediate sense of his body and also help to form some 'here and now' reality contact. *Word-for-Word Reflections* (WWR) mirror back to the person those words, sounds or sentences that are socially comprehensible or which seemed meaningful to the client. These reflections help the client to experience himself once again as an expressor and communicator and in that sense they work towards restoring functional speech. *Reiterative Reflections* (RR) repeat previously successful reflections in order to strengthen the contact established and further facilitate the experiencing process, for example, 'I said "floor" and you looked at me', 'You looked at my watch and I said it was 3 p.m.'

The second level on which contact is described in pre-therapy is as a set of psychological functions necessary for therapy to occur: the *contact functions*. The contact reflections of the therapist are designed to establish, maintain and possibly strengthen the three contact functions in the client. *Reality Contact* (RC) is the client's concrete awareness of people, places, events and things; *Affective Contact* (AC) comprises the client's awareness of emotions, moods and feelings; and *Communicative Contact* (CC) is the client's communication of his awareness of reality and his affect to other people.

The third level at which contact is theoretically described is in terms of the behaviour which the client exhibits as a result of developing the contact functions: this is called *contact behaviour*. As a consequence of developing contact with reality, affective contact and communicative contact the client's level of functioning in life is augmented, helping him or her to engage more fully in social, vocational and educational activities as well as making it possible for him or her to enter psychotherapy eventually.

These contact reflections, contact functions and contact behaviours form the basic concepts of client-centred pre-therapy. Rather than continue with the theoretical exposition, it is perhaps more useful in this introduction to present some clinical illustrations of the use of pre-therapy reflections.

In the hospital where I work, the staff have developed a discipline of reflecting psychotic behaviour whenever possible and when not contra-indicated by their responsibilities for managing the rest of the ward. This means that they try to work from within the client's process rather than being controlling, interpretative or judgemental about the things someone says or does. The use of reflections is a way of meeting clients on their own ground and helping them to make greater contact with reality, with their feelings and with other people.

For example, Christiane walks into the nurses' office, stands still and stares straight ahead. She is obviously in a kind of closed, locked-up position, but nevertheless she has come to the office or to the nurses. Instead of immediately telling her to go back to her room or pedagogically instructing her first to knock on the door and then come in, one of the nurses empathically reflects what is happening: 'You are standing in the office [SR]. You look in the direction of the window [SR]. You are staring [FR].' These reflections seem to enable Christiane to contact her feelings and free herself from whatever had been on her mind in a way that she could not master. She now says: 'I am afraid that my mother is going to die!' Then she turns herself around and walks towards the living room. The semi-psychotic mood is processed and she is once again in control of herself. She thus becomes able to feel and to communicate in a congruent way and she does not ask for further attention. She can take care of herself once again even though the intervention is short and technically simple.

Another example is taken from the weekly patient-staff meeting where approximately 20 people are sitting in a large circle. Suddenly a patient, Thierry, comes in with a Bible in his hand, walks straight up to me, shows me a page and says 'I can make the words change.' I make eye contact, also point at the Bible [BR] and reflect 'I can make the words change [WWR]. Thierry, we are sitting in a circle [SR]. You're standing up [BR] next to me [SR] and are showing me the Bible [RR].' Reflecting all this enables Thierry to realise that he is doing something odd, given the context of the situation, and he is able to anchor himself back into the shared reality by taking a chair and sitting quietly at the edge of the circle.

In another meeting, Chantal suddenly stands up, points at the window and says 'I see them moving again!' I reflect her words (WWR) and also the anxious expression on her face (FR). These interventions seem to restore her ability to make contact and by doing so they bring her out of her psychotic world. She looks around, becomes aware of the group once again, sits down and non-verbally shows that we can go on with the meeting. The group seems relieved that she is with us again and that the psychotic episode has not automatically led to repressive inter-action, but instead has been dealt with in a very accepting, containing way.

Examples such as these can be translated into any other setting and into any relationship between two persons where one is in a vulnerable state and functioning on a pre-expressive level (Prouty, 1998) and the other is empathically present with the intention to enable the first person to come back from contact-loss into the world of feeling and communicating.

Intensive case studies of pre-therapy work are available; for example, Prouty and Cronwal (1989) describe pre-therapy with a depressed profoundly retarded adult; Prouty and Kubiak (1988) illustrate work with a catatonic schizophrenic of high intelligence; and Prouty (1990) presents pre-therapy with a retarded person displaying schizophrenic-like symptoms.

The next section offers a slightly more detailed illustration of pre-therapy working where the practitioner can use the pre-therapy discipline and techniques even when he or she does not know the basis of the client's communication. This offers yet another example of a recurrent theme in this book: that in person-centred working it is much more important to be psychologically 'present' and in 'contact' with the client than actually to understand what the client is communicating.

KEY POINT When working with clients whose communication about reality and feelings is severely impaired, the client-centred 'pre-therapy' methodology of Garry Prouty offers a meaningful system for achieving psychological contact.

Note

In this section and the one which follows the term 'therapist' rather than 'counsellor' has been used in acknowledgement of the language used in the author's work context.

30 Dealing with the possibility of psychotic content in a seemingly congruent communication

DION VAN WERDE

In practical working with, for example, psychiatric hospital patients, it can be difficult to be sure whether the patient is communicating from a psychotic reality or a shared reality. Prouty's pre-therapy reflections provide a useful framework for response because they are both meaningful in terms of a shared reality and also effective in helping the client to restore congruent communication from an initially psychotic reality. The following example gives some detail on how this method of communication offers a considerable resource to psychiatric nursing and medical staff (see also Van Werde and Prouty, 1992), but it can also be learned by community care workers and family carers.

The client, Marianne, walked into the nurses' office and said 'Are they coming to get me?' In that moment I did not know whether psychotic (paranoid) content was being expressed, whether this was congruent, reality-based communication, or maybe even both. This particular level of functioning I elsewhere call grey-zone functioning (Van Werde, 2002). Marianne had been with us for two weeks and I knew that psychosis was never far away. On the other hand, most of the time, congruent communication was possible. So, I was faced with the problem of how to respond to this question. Since reacting to a client always involves a decision, or at least retrospectively we should be able to construct which elements played a role in our decision, I shall share with you what went through my mind and how things proceeded. The mere doubt about her level of functioning (psychotic and/or congruent) made me choose to respond with *contact reflections*. The doubt about her congruence arose when she had entered the office (slowly and more or less staring) and when I had heard her ask the question in a strange and monotone way. At the same time I had seen her quickly look through the window. I had followed her sight and spotted, from the corner of my eye, a bird fly away. The idea crossed my mind that 'coming to get me' could also have something to do with the looking outside and the flying away. If this were so, then Marianne would be functioning on a pre-expressive level and pre-therapy reflections would be indicated. I did not at that moment believe in the necessity of taking over the initiative either to control or to cut through or interrupt the process of this client. I believed that she was trying to communicate to me something of what was going on in her inner world, but probably on a level that is hardly understandable for herself, let alone for an outsider. This woman was struggling with her feelings, struggling with realities and struggling to communicate. What she was saying and doing is thus very loaded with meaning and by definition relevant. However, the only person who could really express, reveal or decode what was going on and which meanings were involved was the client herself. In that moment I chose my intervention to aim at bringing the client back in contact with her process of experiencing so that she could build up her own level of functioning herself. Thus, I responded with *contact reflections* to keep that possibility open.

Dion: Are they coming to get me? [WWR]

> [Since Marianne did not react verbally, but kept staring at me with an unchanged body posture, I tried again to bring her into contact with what was actually happening.]

You look at me [SR] and ask if they are coming to get you [RR].
Marianne: Are they coming to get me?

> [This strengthened my hypothesis that she was in a psychotic state, so I reflected what she did with her body as an extra means for anchorage.]

Dion: Just a second ago you looked up

> [and I myself looked at the window in the same way that she had [BR]],

and asked 'Are they coming to get me?' [RR].
Marianne: I always hear airplanes and things.

> [Obviously she was now showing something of her psychotic world. I maintained eye contact and reflected.]

Dion: I always hear airplanes and things [WWR].
Marianne: What do you think? . . . I want to know.

[I was not clear what she meant by this question. Was she asking my opinion about the situation, the interaction or about airplanes? Does she mean that these things are going to take her away? In that moment I myself experienced the blend of the two worlds: the reality of our conversation and/or the reality of her paranoid psychotic system. All I felt I could do was to reflect her question and hope that she would clarify it to herself and to me.]

Dion: You ask me what I think [WWR].
Marianne: Are they coming to get me?

[I had a very clear feeling that every word was important but I did not know what she was going through or where these words were leading her. I carefully reflected only what she had given thus making sure not to distract her from her own process.]

Dion: Are they coming to get me? [WWR]. Just a while ago you said 'I always hear airplanes and things' [RR]. Now you are looking at me [SR] and ask: 'Are they coming to get me?' [WWR].
Marianne: Can I phone home?

[This was a direct question and I gave a congruent answer since I thought that her level of functioning was more congruent and contact reflections were no longer indicated, so I replied.]

Dion: You already phoned home: what did you agree with them?
Marianne: They are coming at 2 p.m. It's still one and a half hours to wait.

[This was obviously Reality Contact. Her parents were going to pick her up for a weekend leave at 2 p.m. and it was indeed only 12.30 p.m. I continued on a congruent level and made some suggestions.]

Dion: Indeed, so what will you do? Perhaps walk around a bit? Perhaps you could lay down on your bed ...?
Marianne: Not on my bed, otherwise I think they will come and get me. I'm not sure I would survive.

[Probably my suggestions have induced her to become more psychotic once again, so I returned to Word-for-Word Reflection and tried not to go beyond what she gave me since her anchorage was fragile.]

Dion: You don't know if you would survive [WWR]. You say: 'I'm not going to lay down, otherwise I think they will come and get me [RR]'.
Marianne: I don't know if I will be alive.
Dion: You look at me [SR] and say: 'I don't know if I will be alive' [WWR]. Your eyes look sad [FR]. You shiver [BR].
Marianne: I don't feel easy at all.

In this last statement Marianne has contacted her feelings. This is *Affective Contact*. In the interaction which followed, Marianne very adequately talked about her fear of travelling, made a phone call to change the hour of pick-up and empathically understood her mother who tried to reassure her daughter about the pick-up.

This dialogue illustrates the thinking of the practitioner using client-centred pre-therapy methodology in everyday contact with patients. Marianne was helped to change her level of functioning in such a way as to make more contact with her feelings and with the shared reality. This step was made possible through empathic contact with Marianne *at the level on which she was functioning* and with respect for her own tempo.

Clinically, helping this client to come back into 'contact', albeit for a short period of time, appeared to be very relevant. Some weekends earlier, in a moment of contact-loss, she had tried to suffocate her younger brother to prevent him from being murdered also by the people that would 'come to get' her. Later, we heard that there possibly had been an incestuous relationship between her and a male member of her family. This would make it understandable why Marianne came to the edge of psychosis given the uncertainty about when she would be picked up. Also the suggestion to 'lay down on the bed' while waiting to be picked up could very well fit in with the hypothetical traumatic incestuous experiences and thus might have been capable of triggering psychotic experiencing/processing.

This demonstrates that one never knows, and that even the smallest remark coming from outside the frame of reference of the client can be intrusive and can even cause powerful and non-intended anti-therapeutic effects. The client is the one who knows – therefore he has to be the touchstone and cornerstone of all our therapeutic efforts.

> **KEY POINT**   Where the practitioner is unsure about whether the client is communicating from a psychotic or a congruent state, the pre-therapy methodology offers an effective means of operating.

References

American Psychiatric Association (1987) *Diagnostic and Statistical Manual of Mental Disorders (DSM-III-R)* (3rd edn revised). Washington, DC: American Psychiatric Association.

Axline, V. (1964) *Dibs: In Search of Self*. Harmondsworth: Penguin.

BACP (2002) *Counselling and Psychotherapy Research*. Rugby: British Association for Counselling and Psychotherapy.

Baldwin, M. (ed.) (2000) *The Use of Self in Therapy* (2nd edn). New York: The Haworth Press.

Barnes, M. and Berke, J. (1991) *Mary Barnes: Two Accounts of a Journey Through Madness*. London: Free Association Books.

Berghofer, G. (1996) 'Dealing with schizophrenia – a person-centered approach providing care to long-term patients in a supported residential service in Vienna', in R. Hutterer, G. Pawlowsky, P. Schmid and R. Stipsits (eds), *Client-Centered and Experiential Psychotherapy: A Paradigm in Motion*. Frankfurt am Main: Peter Lang. pp. 481–93.

Bettelheim, B. (1987) 'The man who cared for children', *Horizon*. London: BBC Television.

Binder, U. (1998) 'Empathy and empathy development with psychotic clients', in B. Thorne and E. Lambers (eds), *Person-Centred Therapy: a European Perspective*. London: Sage. pp 216–30.

Bohart, A. (1990) 'A cognitive client-centred perspective on borderline personality development', in G. Lietaer, J. Rombauts and R. Van Balen (eds), *Client-Centered and Experiential Psychotherapy in the Nineties*. Leuven: Leuven University Press. pp. 559–621.

Boy, A.V. (1989) 'Psychodiagnosis: a person-centered perspective', *Person-Centered Review*, 4 (2): 132–51.

Bozarth, J. (1984) 'Beyond reflection: emergent modes of empathy', in R. Levant and J. Shlien (eds), *Client-Centered Therapy and the Person-Centered Approach*. New York: Praeger. pp. 59–75.

Bozarth, J. and Temaner Brodley, B. (1986) 'The core values and theory of the person-centered approach', paper presented at the First Annual Meeting of the Association for the Development of the Person-Centered Approach, Chicago.

Coffeng, T. (1996) 'The delicate approach to early trauma', in R. Hutterer, G. Pawlowsky, P. Schmid and R. Stipsits (eds), *Client-Centered and Experientio Psychotherapy: A Paradigm in Motion*. Frankfurt: Peter Lang. pp. 499–51]

Combs, A.W. (1989) *A Theory of Therapy.* Newbury Park, CA: Sage.

Cooper, M. (1999) 'If you can't be Jekyll be Hyde: an existential-phenomenological exploration of lived-plurality', in J. Rowan and M. Cooper (eds), *The Plural Self.* London: Sage. pp. 51–70.

Davies, D. and Neal, C. (eds) (1996) *Pink Therapy: A Guide for Counsellors and Therapists Working with Lesbian, Gay and Bisexual Clients.* Buckingham: Open University Press.

Davies, D. and Neal, C. (eds) (2000) *Therapeutic Perspectives on Working with Lesbian, Gay and Bisexual Clients.* Buckingham: Open University Press.

Dinnage, R. (1987) *One to One: Experiences of Psychotherapy.* London: Viking, Penguin.

Fischer, C. (1987) 'Beyond transference', *Person-Centered Review, 2* (2): 157–64.

Gendlin, E. (1981) *Focusing.* New York: Bantam Books.

Gendlin, E. (1984) 'The client's client: the edge of awareness', in R. Levant and J. Shlien (eds), *Client-Centered Therapy and the Person-Centered Approach.* New York: Praeger. pp. 76–107.

Gendlin, E. T. (1996) *Focusing-Oriented Psychotherapy.* New York: Guilford.

Ginsberg, B. (1984) 'Beyond behaviour modification: client centered play therapy with the retarded', *Academic Psychology Bulletin,* 6 (November).

Goss, S. and Mearns, D. (1997a) 'A call for a pluralist epistemological understanding in the assessment and evaluation of counselling', *British Journal of Guidance and Counselling,* 25 (2): 189–98.

Goss, S. and Mearns, D. (1997b) 'Applied pluralism in the evaluation of employee counselling', *British Journal of Guidance and Counselling,* 25 (3): 327–44.

Heron, J. (1997) 'The politics of transference', in R. House and N. Totton (eds), *Implausible Professions.* Ross-on-Wye: PCCS Books. pp. 11–18.

Kagan, N. (1984) 'Interpersonal process recall: basic methods and recent research', in D. Larson (ed.), *Teaching Psychological Skills: Models for Giving Psychology Away.* Monterey, CA: Brooks/Cole.

Kahn, E. (1987) 'On the therapeutic value of both the "Real" and the "Transference" relationship', *Person-Centered Review, 2* (4): 471–5.

Kirschenbaum, H. and Henderson, V. (1989) *The Carl Rogers Reader.* London: Constable.

Kottler, J. A. and Brown, R. L. (1985) *Introduction to Therapeutic Counselling.* Monterey, CA: Brooks/Cole.

Kroll, J. (1988) *The Challenge of the Borderline Patient.* New York: Norton.

ᵀaing, R.D., Phillipson, H. and Lee, A.R. (1966) *Interpersonal Perception.* London: Tavistock.

ıbers, E. (2000) 'Supervision in person-centred therapy: facilitating ongruence', in D. Mearns and B. Thorne, *Person-Centred Therapy Today: ew Frontiers in Theory and Practice.* London: Sage. pp. 196–211.

ːr, G. (1984) 'Unconditional positive regard: a controversial basic attitude client-centered therapy', in R Levant and J. Shlien (eds), *Client-Centered rapy and the Person-Centered Approach.* New York Praeger. pp. 41–58.

ɪ, J. (1994) *Doing Counselling Research.* London: Sage.

McLeod, J. (1997) *Narrative and Psychotherapy.* London: Sage.

McLeod, J. (1999) *Practitioner Research in Counselling.* London: Sage.

McLeod, J. (2001) *Qualitative Research in Counselling and Psychotherapy.* London: Sage.

McWilliams, K. and Prouty, G. (1998) 'Life enrichment of a profoundly retarded woman: an application of pre-therapy', *The Person-Centered Journal,* 1: 29–35.

Mearns, D. (1989) 'The counsellor's experience of success', in D. Mearns and W. Dryden (eds), *Experiences of Counselling in Action.* London: Sage. pp. 97–112.

Mearns, D. (1991a) 'The unspoken relationship in psychotherapy', The Wellspring Public Lecture, Queen's Hall, Edinburgh, 29 May.

Mearns, D. (1991b) 'On being a supervisor', in B. Thorne and W. Dryden (eds), *Training and Supervision for Counselling in Action.* London: Sage. pp. 116–28.

Mearns, D. (1992a) 'Tapping the unspoken relationship between counsellor and client', paper presented at the Second International Conference on Client-Centred and Experiential Psychotherapy, Stirling, Scotland.

Mearns, D. (1992b) 'Dave Mearns' in W. Dryden (ed.), *Hard-earned Lessons from Counselling in Action.* London: Sage. pp. 69–82.

Mearns, D. (1993a) 'The core conditions' in W. Dryden (ed.), *Questions and Answers on Counselling in Action.* London Sage. pp. 1–4.

Mearns, D. (1993b) 'The dance of psychotherapy', public lecture presented in the University of Athens, 16 December.

Mearns, D. (1994) *Developing Person-Centred Counselling.* London: Sage.

Mearns, D. (1996) 'Working at relational depth with clients in person-centred therapy', *Counselling,* 7(4): 306–11.

Mearns, D. (1997a) *Person-Centred Counselling Training.* London: Sage.

Mearns, D. (1997b) 'Achieving the personal development dimension in professional counsellor training', *Counselling,* 8 (2): 113–20.

Mearns, D. (1999) 'Person-centred therapy with configurations of self', *Counselling,* 10(2): 125–30.

Mearns, D. (2002a) 'Client-centred therapy in the modern era: an expanding theory of therapy'. Paper presented to the 3rd World Congress for Psychotherapy, Vienna, July 14–18.

Mearns, D. (2002b) *Person-Centred Therapy.* Masterclass presented in Liverpool, Leeds, Birmingham and London, March 11–15.

Mearns, D. (2002c) 'Further theoretical propositions in regard to self theory within person-centered therapy', *Person-Centered and Experiential Psychotherapies,* 1 (1 & 2): 14–27.

Mearns, D. and Dryden, W. (1989) *Experiences of Counselling in Action.* London: Sage.

Mearns, D. and Thorne, B. (1988) *Person-Centred Counselling in Action.* London: Sage.

Mearns, D. and Thorne, B. (1999) *Person-Centred Counselling in Action* (2nd edn). London: Sage.

Mearns, D. and Thorne, B. (2000) *Person-Centred Therapy Today: New Frontiers in Theory and Practice.* London: Sage.

Merleau-Ponty, M. (1962) *Phenomenology of Perception*. New York: Routledge & Kegan Paul.

Merry, T. (1990) 'PCA – person-centred anything', *Self and Society*, 18 (1): 35–7.

Neal, C. and Davies, D. (eds) (2000) *Issues in Therapy with Lesbian, Gay, Bisexual and Transgender Clients*. Buckingham: Open University Press.

O'Leary, C. (1999) *Couple and Family Counselling: A Person-Centred Approach*. London: Sage.

Patel, V. and Winston, M. (1994) 'Universality of mental illness: assumptions, artefacts and new directions', *British Journal of Psychiatry*, 165: 437–40

Peters, H. (1999) 'Pre-therapy: a client-centered experiential approach to mentally handicapped people', *Journal of Humanistic Psychology*, 39 (4): 8–29.

Prouty, G.F. (1976) 'Pre-therapy, a method of treating pre-expressive psychotic and retarded patients', *Psychotherapy: Theory, Research and Practice*, 13 (3): 290–5.

Prouty, G.F. (1990) 'A theoretical evolution in the person-centered/experiential psychotherapy of schizophrenia and retardation', in G. Lietaer, J. Rombauts and R. Van Balen (eds), *Client-Centered and Experiential Psychotherapy in the Nineties*. Leuven: Leuven University Press. pp. 645–85.

Prouty, G. F. (1998) 'Pre-therapy and the pre-expressive self', *Person-Centred Practice*, 6 (2): 80–8.

Prouty, G.F. (1994) *Theoretical Evolutions in Person-Centered/Experiential Therapy*. Westport: Praeger.

Prouty, G.F. and Cronwal, M. (1989) 'Psychotherapy with a depressed mentally retarded adult: an application of pre-therapy', in A. Dozen and F. Menolascino, *Depression in Mentally Retarded Children and Adults*. Leiden: Logon Publications. pp. 281–93.

Prouty, G.F. and Kubiak, M.A. (1988) 'The development of communicative contact with a catatonic schizophrenic', *Journal of Communication Therapy*, 4 (1): 13–20.

Prouty, G., F. Van Werde, D. and Portner, M. (forthcoming) *Pre-Therapy*. Ross-On-Wye: PCCS Books.

Raskin, N.J. (1952) 'An objective study of the locus of evaluation factor in psychotherapy', in W. Wolff and J.A. Precker (eds), *Success in Psychotherapy*. New York: Grune & Stratton.

Reid, W. and Wise, M. (1989) *DSM-III-R Training Guide*. New York: Brunner/ Mazel.

Rennie, D. (1984) 'Clients' tape assisted recall of psychotherapy: a qualitative analysis'. Paper presented at the Canadian Psychological Association, Ottawa, 31 May.

Rennie, D. L. (1998) *Person-Centred Counselling: An Experiential Approach*. London: Sage.

Rogers, C.R. (1951) *Client-Centered Therapy*. London: Constable.

Rogers, C.R. (1957) 'The necessary and sufficient conditions of therapeutic personality change', *Journal of Consulting Psychology*, 21 (2): 95–103.

Rogers, C.R. (1959) 'A theory of therapy, personality and interpersonal relationships, as developed in the client-centered framework', in S. Koch (ed.), *Psychology: A Study of A Service*. Volume 3: *Formulations of the Person and the Social Contract*. New York: McGraw-Hill. pp. 184–256.

Rogers, C.R. (1980) *A Way of Being*. Boston: Houghton Mifflin.

Rogers, C.R (1986) 'A client-centered/person-centered approach to therapy', in I. Kutash and A. Wolf (eds), *Psychotherapist's Casebook*. San Francisco: Jossey-Bass. pp. 197–208.

Rogers, C.R., Gendlin, E.T., Kiesler, D.B. and Truax, C.B. (eds) (1967) *The Therapeutic Relationship and its Impact: A Study of Psychotherapy with Schizophrenics*. Madison: University of Wisconsin Press.

Rohde-Dachser, C. (1979) *Das Borderline Syndrom*. Bern: Huber.

Rowan, J. (1990) *Subpersonalities*. London: Routledge.

Roy, B. (1991) 'A client-centered approach to multiple personality and dissociated process', in L. Fusek (ed.), *New Directions in Client-Centered Therapy: Practice with Difficult Populations*. Chicago: Chicago Counseling and Psychotherapy Center. pp. 18–40.

Seeman, J. (1987) 'Transference and psychotherapy', *Person-Centered Review,* 2 (2): 189–95.

Shlien, J. (1984) 'A countertheory of transference', in R. Levant and J. Shlien (eds), *Client-Centered Therapy and the Person-Centered Approach*. New York: Praeger. pp. 153–81.

Strupp, H. (1987) 'Response to "A countertheory of transference" by John M. Shlien', *Person-Centered Review,* 2 (2): 196–202.

Sturdevant, K. (1994) 'Intentions and expectations of members of a large person-centred community group', *Renaissance,* Newsletter of the Association for the Development of the Person Centered Approach, 11 (2): 1–7.

Swildens, H. (1990) 'Client-centered psychotherapy for patients with borderline symptoms', in G. Lietaer, J. Rombauts and R Van Balen (eds), *Client-Centered and Experiential Psychotherapy in the Nineties*. Leuven: Leuven University Press. pp. 623–35.

Swildens, H. (1991) 'De psychopathologie in haar betekenis voor de clientgerichte gesprekstherapie', in H. Swildens, O. de Haas, G. Lietaer and R. Van Balen (eds), *Leerboek Gesprekstherapie*. Amersfoort/Leuven: Acco. pp. 305–31.

Thorne, B. (1987) 'Beyond the core conditions', in W. Dryden (ed.), *Key Cases in Psychotherapy*. London: Croom Helm.

Thorne, B. (2002) *The Mystical Power of Person-Centred Therapy*. London: Whurr Publishers.

Tscheulin, D. (1990) 'Confrontation and non confrontation as differential techniques in differential client centered therapy', in G. Lietaer, J. Rombauts and R. Van Balen (eds), *Client-Centered and Experiential Psychotherapy in the Nineties*. Leuven: Leuven University Press. pp. 327–36.

Van De Veire, C. (1995) 'Steunende en structurerende clientgerichte psychotherapie bij een borderline cliente', in G. Lietaer and M. Van Kalmthout (eds), *Praktijkboek Gesprekstherapie: Psychopathologie en experientiele procesbevordering*. Utrecht: De Tijdstroom. pp. 167–77.

Van Werde, D. (1989) 'Restauratie van het psychologisch contact by acute psychose', *Tijdschrift voor Psychotherapie,* 15 (5): 271–9.

Van Werde, D. (1990) 'Psychotherapy with a retarded, schizoaffective woman: an application of Prouty's pre-therapy', in A. Dozen, A. van Gennep and G. Zwanikken (eds), *Treatment of Mental Illness and Behavioral Disorder in the Mentally Retarded*. Proceedings of the International Congress, 3–4 May.

Van Werde, D. (1992) 'Contact-faciliterend werk op een abdeling psychosenzorg: een vertaling van Prouty's pre-therapie', *Vereniging voor Rogeriaanse Therapie-Periodiek* 4: 3–20.

Van Werde, D. (1998) 'Anchorage as a core concept in working with psychotic people', in B. Thorne and E. Lambers (eds), *Person-Centred Therapy: A European Perspective*. London: Sage. pp. 195–205.

Van Werde, D. (2002) 'The value of Prouty's pre-therapy when working with a broad range of persons' pre-expressive functioning', in G. Wyatt and P. Sanders (eds), *Contact and Perception*. Ross-On-Wye: PCCS Books.

Van Werde, D. and Morton, I. (1999) 'The relevance of Prouty's pre-therapy to dementia care', in I. Morton (ed.), *Person-Centred Approaches to Dementia Care*. Bicester, Oxon: Winslow Press. pp 139–66.

Van Werde, D. and Prouty, G.F. (1992) 'Het herstellen van het psychologisch contact bij een schizofrene jonge vrouw: een toepassing van pre-therapie', *Tijdschrift Klinische Psychologie*, 22 (4): 269–80.

Warner, M. (2000) 'Person-centred therapy at the difficult edge: a developmentally based model of fragile and dissociated process', in D. Mearns and B. Thorne, *Person-Centred Therapy Today: New Frontiers in Theory and Practice*. London: Sage. pp. 144–71.

Warner, M. (2001) 'Empathy, relational depth and difficult client process', in S. Haugh and T. Merry (eds), *Empathy*. Ross-on-Wye: PCCS Books. pp. 181–91.

Warner, M. (2002a) Personal Communication.

Warner, M. (2002b) 'Psychological contact, meaningful process and human nature: a reformulation of person-centred theory', in G. Wyatt and P. Sanders (eds), *Contact and Perception*. Ross-on-Wye: PCCS Books. pp. 76–95.

West, J. (1992) *Child-Centred Play Therapy*. London: Edward Arnold.

Zimring F.M. (1990) 'Cognitive processes as a cause of psychotherapeutic change', in G. Lietaer, J. Rombauts and R Van Balen (eds), *Client-Centered and Experiential Psychotherapy in the Nineties*. Leuven: Leuven University Press. pp. 361–80.

Index

Compiled by INDEXING SPECIALISTS, 202 Church Road, Hove, East Sussex
BN3 2DJ. Tel: 01273 738299. E-mail: richardr@indexing.co.uk. Website:
www.indexing.co.uk